DEFENSE, SECURITY AND STRATEGIES

RISK MANAGEMENT OF NATIONAL SECURITY THREATS

SELECT ISSUES AND TOPICS

DEFENSE, SECURITY AND STRATEGIES

Additional books in this series can be found on Nova's website under the Series tab.

Additional E-books in this series can be found on Nova's website under the E-book tab.

DEFENSE, SECURITY AND STRATEGIES

RISK MANAGEMENT OF NATIONAL SECURITY THREATS

SELECT ISSUES AND TOPICS

GUSTAV KNUDSEN
EDITOR

nova publishers
New York

For permission to use material from this book please contact us:
Telephone 631-231-7269; Fax 631-231-8175
Web Site: http://www.novapublishers.com

Library of Congress Cataloging-in-Publication Data

ISBN: 978-1-62618-701-6

Published by Nova Science Publishers, Inc. † New York

CONTENTS

PREFACE

The United States confronts a wide array of threats at U.S. borders, ranging from terrorists who may have weapons of mass destruction, to transnational criminal smuggling drugs or counterfeit goods, to unauthorized migrants intending to live and work in the United States. Given this diversity of threats, how may Congress and the Department of Homeland Security (DHS) set border security priorities and allocate scarce enforcement resources? In general, DHS's answer to this question is organized around risk management, a process that involves risk assessment and the allocation of resources based on a cost-benefit analysis. DHS employs models to classify threats as relatively high- or low-risk for certain planning and budgeting exercises and to implement certain border security programs. This book examines risk management as it relates to national security threats with a focus on border security; chemical, biological, radiological, and nuclear risk assessments; and the publishing of scientific papers with potential security risks.

Chapter 1 – The United States confronts a wide array of threats at U.S. borders, ranging from terrorists who may have weapons of mass destruction, to transnational criminals smuggling drugs or counterfeit goods, to unauthorized migrants intending to live and work in the United States. Given this diversity of threats, how may Congress and the Department of Homeland Security (DHS) set border security priorities and allocate scarce enforcement resources?

In general, DHS's answer to this question is organized around risk management, a process that involves risk assessment and the allocation of resources based on a cost-benefit analysis. This report focuses on the first part of this process by identifying border threats and describing a framework for understanding risks at U.S. borders. DHS employs models to classify threats as relatively high- or low-risk for certain planning and budgeting exercises and to implement certain border security programs. Members of Congress may wish to use similar models to evaluate the costs and benefits of potential border security policies and to allocate border enforcement resources. This report discusses some of the issues involved in modeling border-related threats.

Understanding border risks begins with identifying key threats. At their roots, border-related threats are closely linked to the flow of people (travelers) and goods (cargo) from one country to another. Any smuggled item or individual hidden among the legitimate flows potentially constitutes a threat to U.S. security or interests.

The *intentions* and *actions* of unauthorized travelers separate them into different threat categories, including terrorists, transnational criminals, and other illegal migrants.

Illegal goods are distinguished by their inherent *legitimacy* or *illegitimacy.* Certain weapons, illegal drugs, and counterfeit goods are always illegal and categorically prohibited, while other goods are legal under most circumstances, but become illegitimate if they are smuggled to avoid enforcement of specific laws, taxes, or regulations.

The risks associated with these diverse types of threats may be modeled as a function of (1) the likelihood that the threat will be realized, and (2) the potential consequences of a given threat. In practice, however, estimating likelihood and evaluating potential consequences are challenging tasks, particularly when it comes to the diversity and complexity of border threats. Assessing border threats is also difficult because terrorists, criminals, and migrants are strategic actors who may adapt to border defenses. This report describes some of these challenges, and suggests questions policymakers may ask to develop their own "maps" of border risks. Several potential border threats are described, and the report summarizes what is known about their likelihood and consequences.

The report concludes by discussing how risk assessment may interact with border security policymaking. Given the uncertainty and the subjective judgments involved in modeling risk, policymakers may struggle to reach a consensus on border priorities. Nonetheless, a systematic approach to studying border threats may help clarify the types of policy tradeoffs lawmakers confront at the border.

Chapter 2 – This doctrine, *Risk Management Fundamentals*, serves as an authoritative statement regarding the principles and process of homeland security risk management and what they mean to homeland security planning and execution. It is intended as the capstone doctrine on risk management for the Department of Homeland Security (DHS). Furthermore, *Risk Management Fundamentals* serves as a foundational document supporting DHS risk management efforts in partnership with the homeland security enterprise.

Risk Management Fundamentals is intended to help homeland security leaders, supporting staffs, program managers, analysts, and operational personnel develop a framework to make risk management an integral part of planning, preparing, and executing organizational missions. The development of homeland security risk management doctrine is an essential element in promoting a risk-informed culture enabling training, capability development, and integration across DHS to strengthen and improve the Nation's security. *Risk Management Fundamentals* articulates a desired end-state that DHS aspires to achieve in promoting risk management.

This doctrine is not a substitute for independent thought or innovation in applying these principles and concepts. Simply reading the doctrine will not make one adept in managing risks, nor will attempting to follow the ideas herein as if they were a checklist; rather, doctrine serves to shape how one thinks about the issues that you are considering and should be applied based on the operating environment. Homeland security practitioners should compare the doctrine herein against their own experience and think about why, when, and how it applies to their situation and area of responsibility.

Chapter 3 – The 2001 anthrax attacks in the United States highlighted the need to develop response plans and capabilities to protect U.S. citizens from chemical, biological, radiological, and nuclear (CBRN) agents. Since 2004, the Department of Homeland Security (DHS) has spent at least $70 million developing more than 20 CBRN risk assessments. GAO was requested to assess, from fiscal year 2004 to the present, the extent to which DHS has used its CBRN risk assessments to inform CBRN response plans and CBRN capabilities, and has institutionalized their use. GAO examined relevant laws, Homeland Security Presidential Directives, an Executive Order, DHS guidance, and all 12 relevant interagency CBRN response plans developed by DHS. Based on a review of a United States governmentwide CBRN database and DHS interviews, among other things, GAO selected a nongeneralizable set of seven DHS capabilities used specifically for detecting or responding to CBRN incidents to identify examples of DHS's use of its CBRN risk assessments. GAO also interviewed relevant DHS officials. This is a public version of a classified report that GAO issued in October 2011. Information DHS deemed sensitive or classified has been redacted.

Chapter 4 – The federal government generally supports the publication of federally funded research results because wide dissemination may drive innovation, job creation, technology development, and the advance of science. However, some research results could also be used for malicious purposes. Congress, the Administration, and other stakeholders, are considering whether current policies concerning publishing such research results sufficiently balances the potential benefits with the potential harms. The current issues under debate cut across traditional policy areas, involving simultaneous consideration of security, scientific, health, export, and international policy. Because of the complexity of these issues, analysis according to one set of policy priorities may adversely affect other policy priorities. For example, maximizing security may lead to detriments in public health and scientific advancement, while maximizing scientific advancement may lead to security risks. Accounting for such trade-offs may allow policymakers to establish regulatory frameworks that more effectively maximize the benefits from dual-use research while mitigating its potential risks.

The current consideration of these issues began in late 2011, when two groups of U.S. government-funded scientists submitted papers to academic journals detailing genetic modifications that increase the transmissibility of a deadly influenza strain. Although these research results may improve pandemic influenza preparedness and response, they may also increase the probability that a highly contagious and deadly influenza strain will be introduced, either accidently or deliberately, into the human population.

Stakeholders, including the Department of Health and Human Services, the World Health Organization, journal publishers, and scientists, debated whether the possible benefits of publication outweighed the potential harms. The editors of the scientific journals decided to publish modified versions of both papers.

The controversy surrounding the publication of these influenza experiments demonstrated flaws in the existing federal mechanisms to identify and balance potential benefits of life science research and security trade-offs. Responding to these cases, the Administration released a new government-wide policy to address some of these flaws. It requires agencies that fund life science research to regularly review research portfolios and develop methods to mitigate security risks.

It is not clear whether Congress will agree with the Administration that the new policy sufficiently addresses all of the dual-use issues brought to light by this recent controversy. Congress could decide to allow the new policy to be fully implemented before evaluating whether it appropriately addresses the policy issues. Alternatively, Congress could require agencies to implement robust processes to identify potential research of concern prior to funding; require federal prepublication review of all potential research of concern to establish appropriate limits on the distribution of the research results; require federal licensing of researchers permitted to conduct such experiments and access results; and limit such research to the most safe and secure laboratories.

This report describes the underlying controversy, the potential benefits and harms of publishing these manuscripts, the actions taken by domestic and international stakeholders, and options to improve the way research is handled to minimize security concerns.

In: Risk Management ...
Editor: Gustav Knudsen
ISBN: 978-1-62618-701-6

Chapter 1

BORDER SECURITY: UNDERSTANDING THREATS AT U.S. BORDERS*

Marc R. Rosenblum, Jerome P. Bjelopera and Kristin M. Finklea

SUMMARY

The United States confronts a wide array of threats at U.S. borders, ranging from terrorists who may have weapons of mass destruction, to transnational criminals smuggling drugs or counterfeit goods, to unauthorized migrants intending to live and work in the United States. Given this diversity of threats, how may Congress and the Department of Homeland Security (DHS) set border security priorities and allocate scarce enforcement resources?

In general, DHS's answer to this question is organized around risk management, a process that involves risk assessment and the allocation of resources based on a cost-benefit analysis. This report focuses on the first part of this process by identifying border threats and describing a framework for understanding risks at U.S. borders. DHS employs models to classify threats as relatively high- or low-risk for certain planning and budgeting exercises and to implement certain border security programs. Members of Congress may wish to use similar models to evaluate the costs and benefits of potential border security policies and to allocate

* This is an edited, reformatted and augmented version of Congressional Research Service, Publication No. R42969, dated February 21, 2013.

border enforcement resources. This report discusses some of the issues involved in modeling border-related threats.

Understanding border risks begins with identifying key threats. At their roots, border-related threats are closely linked to the flow of people (travelers) and goods (cargo) from one country to another. Any smuggled item or individual hidden among the legitimate flows potentially constitutes a threat to U.S. security or interests.

The *intentions* and *actions* of unauthorized travelers separate them into different threat categories, including terrorists, transnational criminals, and other illegal migrants.

Illegal goods are distinguished by their inherent *legitimacy* or *illegitimacy*. Certain weapons, illegal drugs, and counterfeit goods are always illegal and categorically prohibited, while other goods are legal under most circumstances, but become illegitimate if they are smuggled to avoid enforcement of specific laws, taxes, or regulations.

The risks associated with these diverse types of threats may be modeled as a function of (1) the likelihood that the threat will be realized, and (2) the potential consequences of a given threat. In practice, however, estimating likelihood and evaluating potential consequences are challenging tasks, particularly when it comes to the diversity and complexity of border threats. Assessing border threats is also difficult because terrorists, criminals, and migrants are strategic actors who may adapt to border defenses. This report describes some of these challenges, and suggests questions policymakers may ask to develop their own "maps" of border risks. Several potential border threats are described, and the report summarizes what is known about their likelihood and consequences.

The report concludes by discussing how risk assessment may interact with border security policymaking. Given the uncertainty and the subjective judgments involved in modeling risk, policymakers may struggle to reach a consensus on border priorities. Nonetheless, a systematic approach to studying border threats may help clarify the types of policy tradeoffs lawmakers confront at the border.

INTRODUCTION

America's borders and ports are busy places, with tens of millions of cargo containers and hundreds of millions of lawful travelers entering the country each year,[1] while tens of thousands of illegal cargo entries and hundreds of thousands of unauthorized migrants are seized, arrested, or turned away.[2] At the same time, hundreds of thousands of unauthorized migrants evade detection to enter the United States illegally;[3] thousands of kilograms of illegal drugs and other contraband are smuggled into the country;[4] and tens of thousands of migrants may be victims of human trafficking.[5] The breadth and variety of these statistics are reflected in the Department of Homeland Security's (DHS's) complex border security mission, which calls on the agency to "prevent the illegal flow of people and goods across U.S. air, land, and sea borders while expediting the safe flow of lawful travel and commerce; ensure security and resilience of global movement systems; [and] disrupt and dismantle transnational organizations that engage in smuggling and trafficking across the U.S. border."[6]

To execute this mission successfully, DHS and Congress must balance a number of competing priorities and allocate resources accordingly. For example, how should enforcement programs weigh the facilitation of legal trade and travel against the competing goal of preventing illegal entries? How should the allocation of border security resources be divided among programs designed to counter differing threats? Is it more efficient to invest enforcement dollars at ports of entry or on fencing and surveillance between the ports? Should additional personnel be added to the Southwest border or at Northern or coastal borders? How do intelligence operations and cooperation with enforcement agencies away from the border enhance border security?

The answers to these questions depend on the variety of threats America confronts at its international borders. DHS and its congressional supporters may have had the luxury of adopting an "all of the above" approach in the years following the September 11, 2001 (9/11), terrorist attacks; but at a time of fiscal scarcity the department faces increasing pressure to invest prudently, and to ensure that effective enforcement strategy shapes agency budgets rather than the other way around.[7] In addition, because many threat actors are strategic (i.e., they may change their tactics in response to enforcement efforts), questions about the effectiveness of U.S. border security policy and the costs and benefits of competing approaches should be revisited on a regular basis.

In general, DHS's border enforcement strategy, like its overall approach to homeland security, is based on risk management, which DHS defines as "the process for identifying, analyzing, and communicating risk and accepting, avoiding, transferring, or controlling it to an acceptable level considering associated costs and benefits of any actions taken."[8] In short, the goal of risk management is to target enforcement resources to specific threats in proportion (1) to the gravity of the associated risk, and (2) to the cost-effectiveness of the enforcement response.

This report focuses on the first major step in managing border-related risks: assessing the risk posed by different types of threats at U.S. borders. Risk assessment in the border security context presents particular challenges, as discussed below (see "A Framework for Assessing Border Threats"). But understanding these challenges and systematically assessing border threats provide a critical foundation for DHS's planning process, as well as for Members of Congress charged with making border security policy, overseeing enforcement efforts, and allocating agency resources.

This report begins with a discussion of the types of threats the United States confronts at its international borders (see "Types of Border Threats"), followed by an overview of DHS's risk management methodologies, including in the context of border security (see "DHS and Risk Management"). The following sections show how the principles of risk management may be used to describe and analyze threats to U.S. border security. First, how can Members of Congress and others assess the risks associated with each of these threats (see "A Framework for Assessing Border Threats")? Second, for selected border threats, what conclusions may be drawn about current risk levels (see "Assessment of Selected Border Threats")? The report concludes by placing threat assessment within the broader context of border security policymaking.

TYPES OF BORDER THREATS

America's concern for national security at the border long predates the post-9/11 focus on "homeland security,"[9] though the nature of border threats has changed over time. The first federal immigration laws, passed in 1798, authorized the President to arrest or deport any alien deemed to be dangerous to the United States and any adult male alien from a country at war with the United States.[10] Over the course of the 20th century, laws were passed to exclude security threats such as anarchists (in 1903), aliens considered a threat to public safety during times of war (1918), communists (1950), and terrorists (1996).[11]

The mission and focus of U.S. border enforcement has also changed over time. The U.S. Border Patrol (USBP) was established in 1924 and focused initially on preventing the entry of inadmissible Chinese migrants and on preventing alcohol inflows during Prohibition, with the majority of agents stationed on the Northern border.[12] Unauthorized migration from and through Mexico first emerged as a major policy concern beginning in the late 1960s and early 1970s,[13] and 1971 marked the beginning of tightening border controls as part of America's "war on drugs."

Thus, beginning in the 1970s, the United States engaged in sustained and intertwined efforts to combat illegal migration and drug flows at the Southwest border.[14] Border patrol staffing (focused primarily on immigration control) climbed eleven-fold between 1975 and 2011,[15] and spending by the Drug Enforcement Administration (DEA, focused primarily on counter-narcotics) increased about five-fold during the same period.[16]

With the first World Trade Center bombing in 1993 and the interception of the so-called millennium bomber at Port Angeles, WA, in 1999, counterterrorism became a third important focus of U.S. border security (i.e., in addition to immigration control and counter-narcotics) during the 1990s—and the top concern after 9/11. Thus, DHS's border security responsibilities were defined by the Homeland Security Act (HSA, P.L. 107-296) to include, among other responsibilities, preventing the entry of terrorists and terrorist weapons; securing U.S. borders, territorial waters, ports, and transportation systems; immigration enforcement; and customs enforcement (including preventing the entry of illegal drugs).[17]

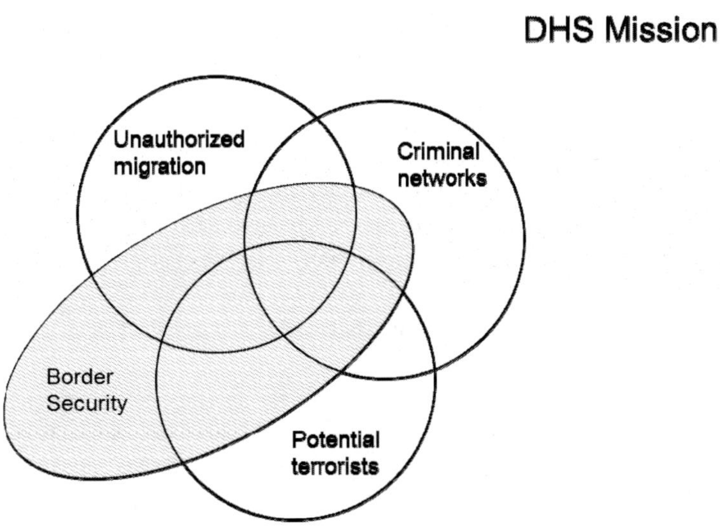

Source: CRS Analysis.

Notes: Figure is schematic. "Unauthorized migration," "criminal networks," and "potential terrorists" are not scaled to suggest that they are equally significant.

Figure 1. Border Threats and DHS Mission.

As Figure 1 illustrates, DHS's border security mission includes its efforts to prevent the entry of unauthorized migrants, combat criminal networks that smuggle drugs and other contraband, and identify and interdict potential terrorists at America's borders. The figure also illustrates several observations about the broader context in which these enforcement efforts occur. First, while migration, drugs, and terrorism are DHS's highest-profile concerns at U.S. borders, border security encompasses a number of additional goals, including efforts to facilitate lawful travel and trade and to prevent the entry of persons with serious communicable diseases.[18] These additional aspects of border security are mainly beyond the scope of this report. Second, while DHS combats illegal migration, criminal networks, and potential terrorists at U.S. borders, its work on all three of these issues also extends beyond the border, both within the United States and through international partnerships. Third, DHS's efforts at U.S. borders and its efforts to combat unauthorized migration, drugs and criminal networks, and terrorism represent a subset of the department's overall homeland security mission space, as illustrated by the larger rectangle in Figure 1. A final observation illustrated by Figure 1 is that while the different elements of DHS's border security mission overlap, they also include distinct regions. For example, the "criminal networks" circle in Figure 1 includes characteristics of this threat that are unique to it. Trafficking organizations that specialize in specific crimes fall in this region of the diagram. The circle intersects with "unauthorized migrants," describing possible ways in which these two threats relate, such as drug trafficking organizations that expand into migrant smuggling. At the core of the diagram all three circles overlap and highlight arenas in which the threats converge—drug smugglers, unauthorized aliens, and terrorists may use the same smuggling routes or techniques, for example.

Are Unauthorized Migrants Border Security "Threats"?

Some people may object to describing unauthorized migrants as "threats to border security" because most unauthorized migrants do not intend to harm the United States and generally do not commit non-immigration-related crimes. Nonetheless, this report includes unauthorized migration among the key threats to U.S. border security because even if people disagree about whether unauthorized migrants threaten U.S. economic and security interests, unauthorized migration undoubtedly has a wide range of social, cultural, environmental, and other impacts on the United States.

How people evaluate these diverse effects and the weight they attach to them are inherently subjective (see "Evaluating Potential Consequences of Border Threats"). The public discourse about this issue makes it clear that some Americans view illegal migration as threatening.

In addition, given that DHS's mission includes preventing the entry of terrorists, illegal drugs and contraband, *and unauthorized migrants*, it is useful to understand how the risks associated with each of these inflows overlap—as well as the differences among them—in order to make homeland security policy and allocate agency resources.

While one may be drawn to the core of Figure 1, the peripheral areas of each circle are important because threats encompass distinct features, and certain policy responses may be more appropriate to combat particular threats. For example, while there likely is some degree of overlap among unauthorized migrants, drug smugglers, and potential terrorists as threat issues, the great majority of unauthorized migrants do not fall into the other categories. None of the 9/11 hijackers or known post-9/11 terrorist threats (e.g., Richard Reid, the "shoe bomber"; Umar Farouk Abdulmutallab, the "underwear bomber"; and Faisal Shahzad, the "Times Square bomber") entered the United States illegally. Likewise, while most unauthorized migrants enter the country between ports of entry or by overstaying nonimmigrant visas,[19] many illicit drugs are smuggled into the United States hidden within cargo containers, private vehicles, or in other non-commercial vehicles.[20] As a result, the enforcement tools targeting illegal migration—personnel and infrastructure between ports of entry, worksite enforcement, and visa overstay analysis—likely do little to reduce narcotic smuggling, and vice versa. Another set of enforcement measures may be ideally designed to combat terrorism, and yet another to prevent other border threats, such as fraudulent goods.

In general, border threats may be divided into *actors* and *goods*. Threat actors include potential terrorists, transnational criminals, and unauthorized migrants (see text box), among other types of people whose entry into the United States may produce harmful consequences. Threatening goods include weapons of mass destruction (WMD) and certain other weapons, illegal drugs and other contraband, counterfeit products, and products brought into the United States illegally and/or with potentially harmful effect. While risk management methodologies may be used to analyze a wide variety of threats, this report focuses exclusively on physical threats at U.S. borders, including the inflow of dangerous and/or illegal people and goods.[21]

Threat Actors

Any person who intends to harm the United States, or whose presence may lead to harmful consequences, may be considered a threat and a potential target for border enforcement policies. At least three distinct types of threat actors may be described: transnational terrorists, transnational criminals, and unauthorized migrants. Although certain actors fall into more than one category (e.g., transnational criminals who migrate illegally; transnational terrorists who commit crimes), from an analytic standpoint—and for purposes of designing countermeasures— these actors may be distinguished and categorized by their motives and their behavior.

Transnational Terrorists

The Immigration and Nationality Act (INA) prohibits the admission of any alien who has engaged in a terrorist activity, is considered likely to engage in terrorist activity, has incited terrorist activity, or is a representative of a terrorist organization or a group that endorses or espouses terrorist activity.[22]

A defining feature of terrorists, as distinct from transnational criminals (see "Transnational Criminals"),[23] is that terrorists are motivated by particular grievances[24] about aspects of the societies that surround them, and they articulate their views "on moral grounds."[25] To help explain or contextualize their grievances, terrorists adopt extremist ideologies or narratives.[26] Based on their grievances and ideologies, terrorists generally have goals other than personal monetary gain, which may include both immediate goals that "can be met without overthrowing the political system" and "transformational" goals, such as the destruction of an entire political or economic system.[27]

The INA describes a variety of specific terrorist activities, including the hijacking or sabotage of any conveyance, the seizure or threatened violence against another individual in order to compel a third person or governmental organization to do or abstain from an activity, violence against an internationally protected person, assassination, and the use of a weapon of mass destruction or other dangerous device other than for personal monetary gain.[28] Terrorists often seek to instill fear among a targeted population to "destroy the collective confidence individuals invest in social institutions and ... national leadership."[29] Terrorists use violent tactics to direct public attention toward their grievances, gain recruits, or coerce people.[30] Terrorists also promote their causes by fashioning propaganda.

Transnational Criminals

The INA also prohibits the admission of certain criminals, including aliens who have committed crimes of moral turpitude,[31] aliens with multiple serious criminal convictions, controlled substance traffickers, aliens engaged in prostitution or commercialized vice, significant traffickers in persons, and money launderers, among others.[32]

In contrast with terrorists, criminals generally are non-ideological, and fundamentally motivated by the pursuit of profit.[33] People also participate in criminal organizations for reasons that involve other sorts of personal gain. They may believe, for example, that being a gangster confers a positive social image, or they may desire the "sensation of belonging to a powerful and even prestigious entity."[34] Criminal gangs like MS-13 (Mara Salvatrucha) attract youth by glorifying gang life and by offering a sense of belonging, and the gang also provides membership incentives such as drugs, alcohol, and sex.[35] Additionally, kinship, ethnic ties, or friendship can also play a role in the formation of criminal groups.[36]

Profit incentives drive criminals to "provide goods and services that are either illegal, regulated, or in short supply."[37] They devote resources to enhancing their market-related activities, which can involve carving out and defending turf, devising novel smuggling techniques, running and protecting supply chains, eliminating rivals, laundering money, and shielding their secrets from "competitors" (such as rival gangs and law enforcement).[38] Thus, criminal earnings depend on defying the rule of law, but not necessarily affecting it via revolution.[39] Violence—or its threatened use—plays a key role in the efforts of organized criminals to generate profits. This violence can send a specific message to rivals or enemies—for example about control of markets and supply routes or questions of reputation and status—but it is rarely ideologically driven.[40] In addition, criminals may secure access to illegal markets by corrupting or intimidating public officials, gaining influence over state activity, or even having states co-opt criminals, themselves.[41]

Unauthorized Migrants

In addition to terrorists and certain criminals, the INA defines as inadmissible, among others, aliens with certain health-related concerns, aliens who raise certain foreign policy concerns, aliens considered likely to become a public charge, certain employment-based immigrants who have not received a labor certification, and aliens arriving at an illegal time or place or not in possession of a valid unexpired visa or other valid entry document.[42]

Unauthorized migrants—like legal migrants—may be motivated by some combination of employment opportunities, a general desire to improve their economic circumstances, family connections, and dangerous or difficult conditions in their home countries, among other factors.[43] Apart from immigration-related offenses such as illegal entry[44] or the use of fraudulent documents to obtain employment, many unauthorized aliens never commit a criminal offense,[45] though some unauthorized migrants become involved with transnational criminals during the course of their migration or while obtaining employment.[46]

Thus, while a terrorist may be unauthorized, "regular" unauthorized aliens are distinguished from terrorists in that they are not motivated by extremist ideologies and do not engage in terrorist activities. And, unlike criminals (who also may be unauthorized), "regular" unauthorized aliens do not seek to profit by exploiting illegal markets or providing illegal services, and they do not use violence or the threat of violence to generate profits. (For analytic purposes, this report classifies a terrorist or transnational criminal who migrates illegally to the United States as a terrorist or criminal, respectively, reserving the label of "unauthorized aliens/migrants" for people who have no terrorist or criminal intent.) The key differences among terrorists, transnational criminals, and unauthorized migrants are summarized in Figure 2; the threats associated with these different types of border flows are discussed below (see "Evaluating Potential Consequences of Border Threats").

Illegal Goods

Any good that is smuggled into or out of the United States is illegal and may pose security risks. Illegal goods fall into two broad categories distinguished by their inherent *illegitimacy*: certain weapons, illegal drugs, and counterfeit goods are always illegal and categorically prohibited, while other goods are generally legal, but become illegitimate because they are smuggled to avoid the enforcement of specific laws, taxes, or regulations.

Categorically Prohibited

U.S. law enforcement seeks to prevent a variety of illegal goods from entering the United States. DHS, for instance, has identified "high-consequence weapons of mass destruction (WMD)" as one of the primary threats to homeland security.[47] WMD may come in many forms, and the term often covers chemical, biological, radiological, nuclear, and explosive (CBRNE) weapons.[48]

Terrorists	Transnational Criminals	Unauthorized Migrants
Motivations—*Ideological*—Achieve socially transformative change or narrower, specific ends. Typically not focused on controlling turf or underground markets but react to particular grievances.	**Motivations**—*Profit Driven*—Create and maintain illicit wealth and prestige. Defend criminal markets and turf. Stave off "enemies" including law enforcement, other state actors, and rival criminal groups.	**Motivations**—*Personal Opportunity*—Some combination of factors such as employment opportunities, a general desire to improve their economic circumstances, family connections, and dangerous or difficult conditions in their home countries.
Means—*Propaganda and Violence Featuring Symbolic Dimension*—Justify violence in moral terms. Intend it to restore a particular sense of justice in a society perceived as unjust. Propaganda used to justify cause, recruit and raise support.	**Means**—*Engage in Violence and Corruption Aimed at Goals Tied to Illicit Markets*—Use violence to intimidate officials and rivals to protect operations. Corrupt public officials and people in the private sector. Use violence to exploit innocent victims. Tend to act in obscurity. Occasionally use propaganda to besmirch rivals.	**Means**—*Illegal Entry or Visa Overstay*—Apart from immigration-related offenses such as illegal entry or the use of fraudulent documents to obtain employment, most unauthorized aliens never commit a criminal offense. Some become involved with transnational criminals during the course of their migration or while obtaining employment.

Source: CRS analysis.

Figure 2. Types of Threat Actors.

Concerns over WMD or their component materials crossing the border into the United States generally emphasize terrorists' use of these weapons, yet some have raised concerns that criminal networks may—for the right price—attempt to smuggle WMD or related materials.[49]

In addition to the smuggling of weapons into the United States, there are also border security and national security concerns over the smuggling of weapons *out* of the United States. One such concern involves Mexican drug trafficking organizations purchasing firearms in the United States and smuggling these weapons to Mexico, where their possession by civilians is largely prohibited.[50] Firearms smuggled from the United States into Mexico have been cited as helping to fuel the drug trafficking-related violence in Mexico.[51] Illegal drugs comprise another set of illicit goods that challenges U.S. border security. The United States, through the Controlled Substances Act (CSA, 21 U.S.C. §801 et. seq.), prohibits the possession, production, distribution, and trafficking of a number of drugs and substances. Nonetheless, drug demand in the United States fuels a multi-billion dollar illicit industry, and many of the drugs consumed in the United States are produced internationally and smuggled into the country. As such, illegal drugs are among the top categories of seizures by border security officials. Customs and Border Protection seized an average of 13,717 pounds of drugs each day in FY2011.[52] The smuggling of counterfeit and pirated goods into the United States—particularly by transnational criminal organizations—has also been identified as a threat to border security.[53] This smuggling violates intellectual property rights (IPR) and "threaten[s] America's economic vitality and national security, and the American people's health and safety."[54] In FY2011, Immigration and Customs Enforcement and CBP had 24,792 seizures of counterfeit goods—25% more than in FY2010. The domestic value[55] of these seizures was more than $178 million. Products originating from China—both Mainland China and Hong Kong—accounted for 80% of the products seized.[56]

Illegal via Smuggling

Goods that *are not* categorically prohibited are illegal if they are smuggled into or out of the United States. These otherwise-legitimate goods can pose a variety of threats when they are moved through illicit channels and means. For instance, alcohol, while generally legal and regulated in the United States and other countries, is smuggled to circumvent taxes or to evade laws prohibiting alcohol. One snapshot of alcohol-linked financial losses comes from Michigan, where illegal alcohol imports are estimated to cost the state at least $14 million per year in lost taxes, not including sales tax or business income tax.[57] Cigarettes and other tobacco products are similarly smuggled to circumvent taxes and regulations. Cigarettes, which comprise about 80% of the value of tobacco product shipments in the United States,[58] are smuggled internationally, including to and from the United States, as well as across state lines. Proceeds from the smuggling of cigarettes have been linked to the financing of terrorist operations abroad.[59]

Federal authorities have noted the threats from the movement of illicit proceeds across U.S. borders. Cross-border movement of money is not inherently illegal, but certain practices are. For instance, bulk cash smuggling[60] is one of the primary means by which criminals move their illicit proceeds out of the United States.[61] Estimates are that between $20 billion and $25 billion in bank notes may be smuggled across the Southwest border into Mexico each year.[62] In FY2011, CBP seized an average of $345,687 in undeclared or illicit currency each day—over $126 million total.[63]

A FRAMEWORK FOR ASSESSING BORDER THREATS

The diversity of border threats and the complexity of DHS's border security and border management mission create challenges for border security policymaking and planning. These challenges are amplified by the uncertainty and fear surrounding many border threats. Rather than attempting specific predictions about where, when, and how border threats will be realized, DHS and other analysts often rely on *risk management* as an approach to border security, and on probabilistic *risk models* as a framework for analyzing and describing different types of potential threats.

Risk management and risk assessment procedures are rooted in economic theories of consumer behavior and formal models of decision-making that are used in a wide range of industrial, environmental, business, legal, and other settings. "Risk management" refers to a variety of methodologies for choosing the optimal response to a potentially hazardous situation by comparing the costs and benefits of possible interventions with the expected value of projected outcomes. A specialized school of decision theory known as "probabilistic risk assessment" (PRA) was developed during the 1960s and 1970s to focus on high-consequence, low-probability risks associated with nuclear power plants and other dangerous industrial processes; PRA has influenced some of DHS's thinking on how to respond to the risk of terrorism.[64]

DHS and Risk Management

Within a few years of the 9/11 attacks and the establishment of DHS, the department began to adopt a "risk-based" approach for certain planning and resource allocation purposes.[65] One of the first DHS programs to employ the vocabulary of risk management was the Homeland Security Grant Program (HSGP), managed by the Federal Emergency Management Agency (FEMA).[66] Pursuant to the USA PATRIOT Act of 2001 (P.L. 107-56) and the Homeland Security Act of 2002 (HSA, P.L. 107-296), as amended, DHS is charged with developing a risk assessment formula that is used to distribute a portion of HSGP funds. For FY2012, the HSGP State Homeland Security Program and Urban Areas Security Initiative target funds to states and metropolitan areas, respectively, based on DHS's determination of the risk to these geographic areas and of the anticipated effectiveness of proposed responses.[67]

Another long-standing DHS program relying on risk management is CBP's Automated Targeting System (ATS), which is founded on rules-based cargo screening systems originally deployed by the legacy U.S. Customs Service.

Under the system, electronic cargo and passenger manifests, vehicle crossing records, nonimmigrant entry records, and other information are checked against CBP's National Targeting Center (NTC) and other intelligence and law enforcement databases.

Every traveler, vehicle, and cargo container is assigned a risk score based on a variety of threat scenarios to identify potential terrorist and criminal threats.

Travelers with risk scores above a certain threshold are automatically targeted for secondary inspection at a port of entry.[68]

Pursuant to the Project BioShield Act of 2004 (P.L. 108-276) and a set of White House directives,[69] DHS also has worked with the intelligence community, other federal agencies, and academia to develop formal, quantitative models to assess the risks of possible terrorist attacks using chemical, biological, radiological, or nuclear (CBRN) weapons.

These models, known as the Bioterrorism Risk Assessment (BTRA), the Chemical Terrorism Risk Assessment (CTRA), the Radiological and Nuclear Terrorism Risk Assessment (RNTRA), and the Integrated Terrorism Risk Assessment (ITRA), use PRA "event trees"[70] to estimate the likelihood and potential consequences of millions of different attack scenarios.[71]

The current versions of the four threat assessments were published in 2010-2011, and DHS plans to publish updates every four years, with the next BTRA, CTRA, and NRTRA due in 2014, and the next ITRA due in 2015.[72]

DHS also led the 2011 Strategic National Risk Assessment (SNRA), executed in support of a White House directive to develop an all-hazards national preparedness system.[73]

The SNRA drew on data from existing government assessments, historical records, and judgments from experts in a variety of disciplines to evaluate the risk of various national-level events, including certain natural disasters, technological/accidental hazards, and adversarial/human-caused attacks.[74]

The assessment was limited to "events that have a distinct beginning and end," and therefore excluded, among other threats, "chronic societal concerns, such as immigration and border violations."[75]

Pursuant to the Implementing Recommendations of the 9/11 Commission Act of 2007 (9/11 Act, P.L. 110-53), DHS published its first Quadrennial Homeland Security Review Report (QHSR) in 2010, outlining a homeland security strategy and priority mission areas for DHS and the entire national homeland security enterprise.[76]

The QHSR identifies a wide range of threats, hazards, and other challenges that homeland security policy seeks to address, including WMD, terrorist networks, smuggling, and other illegal flows of people and goods, among others.[77]

CBP and the U.S. Border Patrol (USBP), located within CBP, incorporate principles of risk management in key border security planning documents. CBP's 2009-2014 strategic plan identifies a broad set of potential border risks, including "criminal and terrorist exploitation of international passenger and commercial cargo transportation systems.... [and] the illegal flow of people and contraband" between ports of entry.[78]

CBP's specific objectives, or policy strategies, include "risk management" to secure the nation's borders and using a "risk-based approach" to ensure the efficient flow of lawful trade and travel.[79] Similarly, while earlier U.S. Border Patrol strategic plans had focused on the acquisition of additional border enforcement resources,[80] the USBP's 2012-2016 strategic plan places greater emphasis on the agency's use of risk management principles to shift existing resources among different border sectors in response to evolving threat landscapes.[81]

The most comprehensive statements of DHS's approach to risk management are its *Risk Lexicon*[82] (also see text box, below) and its *Risk Management Fundamentals*.[83]

The *Risk Lexicon* was produced by the DHS Risk Steering Committee, which was formed with membership from across the department "to leverage the risk management capabilities of the DHS Components and to advance Departmental efforts toward integrated risk management."

The lexicon provides "a set of official terms and definitions to ease and improve the communication of risk-related issues for DHS and its partners."[84] *Risk Management Fundamentals* is intended to "promote a common understanding of, and approach to, risk management; to establish organizational practices that should be followed by DHS components; [and] to provide a foundation for conducting risk assessments and evaluating risk management options," among other purposes.[85] To this end, the document describes a six-step DHS risk management process: (1) define the decision-making context; (2) identify potential risks; (3) assess and analyze risks; (4) develop alternatives; (5) decide upon and implement risk management strategies; and (6) evaluate and monitor outcomes.[86]

Understanding Risk: Key Terms

Consequence: Effect of an event, incident, or occurrence.

Likelihood: Chance of something happening, whether defined, measured or estimated objectively or subjectively, or in terms of general descriptors (such as rare, unlikely, likely, almost certain), frequencies, or probabilities.

Risk: Potential for an unwanted outcome resulting from an incident, event, or occurrence, as determined by its likelihood and the associated consequences.

Risk Management: process of identifying, analyzing, assessing, and communicating risk and accepting, avoiding, transferring, or controlling it to an acceptable level at an acceptable cost.

Scenario: Hypothetical situation comprised of a hazard, an entity impacted by that hazard, and associated conditions including consequences when appropriate.

Threat: Natural or man-made occurrence, individual, entity, or action that has or indicates the potential to harm life, information, operations, the environment, and/or property.

Source: DHS Risk Lexicon 2010.

Risk Assessment

Risk management—like almost any process for responding to external threats—involves developing a model of risk assessment.

The standard components of many risk models include estimates of the *likelihood* of a threat (or other adverse event) and the potential *consequence* of the threat.

Risk models based on likelihood and consequences describe risk as a positive function of these two components, so that risk increases with the likelihood and potential consequences associated with a given threat (see Figure 3).

Put another way, this model of risk may be understood as "the statistical expect[ed] value of an unwanted event that may or may not occur."[87]

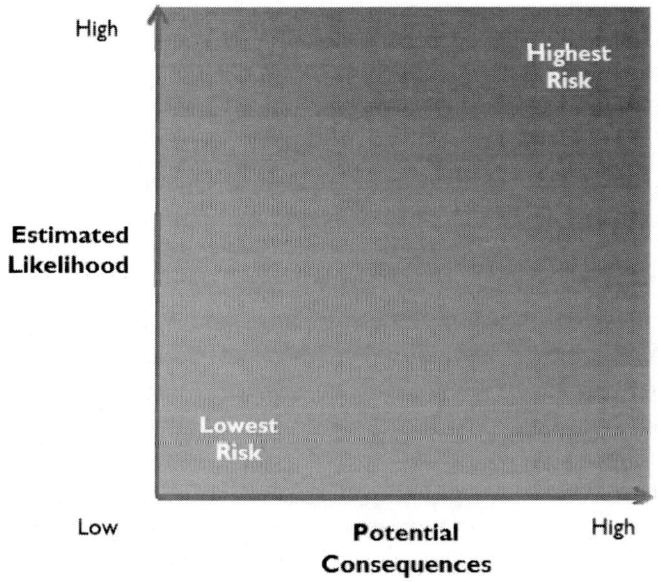

Source: CRS analysis of DHS, *Risk Management Fundamentals* and other risk models.

Figure 3. Two-Dimensional Risk Space.

Thus, as Figure 3 illustrates, events that are unlikely to occur, and that would have low consequences if they did occur, are low-risk threats. Conversely, an event that is likely to occur, and whose occurrence would have severe consequences, would be an especially high-risk threat. Many threats exist between these two extremes, and many threats may be located at other points in Figure 3, including at points near the upper-left corner (i.e., high-likelihood, low-consequence threats) and lower-right corner (i.e., low-likelihood, high-consequence threats).

Several DHS risk assessments adopt some form of this likelihood-times-consequences framework for estimating risk. The HSGP has used several different formulas to calculate the risk to different geographic areas and assets, initially defining risk in terms of population; then by the sum of threat, critical infrastructure, and population density; then by the product of the threat to a target or area, the vulnerability of the target/area, and the consequence of an attack on that target/area.[88] The BTRA, CTRA, NRTRA, and ITRA calculate the risk of various scenarios by multiplying the product of each event tree branch's combined probability by the estimated consequences associated with that branch.[89] And the SNRA, similarly, assessed risk by asking "with what function is it estimated that an event will occur, and what are the consequences of the incident(s) if it does occur?"[90]

DHS has led or conducted risk assessments for a variety of homeland security threats, but existing DHS and CBP strategic documents do not describe and analyze the full range of threats at U.S. borders.[91] The absence of such overarching planning documents may contribute to disagreements about border security priorities: How should CBP and other enforcement agencies prioritize the often conflicting goals of preventing illegal flows versus facilitating lawful trade and travel? How should scarce resources be divided among ports of entry versus the areas between the ports, and among the different border zones? Should the United States use its scarce resources to build additional miles of border fencing, install more surveillance equipment, or hire additional border patrol agents? Is the border really more secure in 2013 than at any time in the past several decades,[92] and what metrics should Congress and DHS use to measure border security?

Some Members of Congress have expressed frustration about the absence of clear border metrics,[93] and some have called for DHS to develop an explicit border staffing model and a comprehensive strategy to secure the border.[94] Risk management offers a *possible* framework for answering these questions and meeting these planning requirements. Understanding border threats can be a logical starting point for this process. This report does not intend to suggest that these are the only ways to examine these issues, however.

UNDERSTANDING BORDER THREATS

The likelihood-times-consequences framework is a standard way to evaluate risk, but the use of such a framework to understand border threats presents unique challenges and therefore remains somewhat controversial.[95] Even where such models are well developed, as in industrial engineering and the insurance and finance industries for example, risk projections are probabilistic and may have a high degree of uncertainty. Predicting the likelihood of border threats may be far more difficult. Moreover, traditional risk management approaches were designed as unilateral decision systems. Yet when it comes to border security, risk models must accommodate strategic adversaries:[96] threat actors like terrorists, criminals, and unauthorized migrants, who may change their behavior in response to U.S. defenses, making likelihood even more difficult to predict. In addition, whereas traditional risk models are designed primarily to measure economic and physical consequences of certain events, the consequences of border threats may affect American society in much more complex ways; and the evaluation of such consequences is likewise more complex. The remainder of this report explores these challenges, and then uses the likelihood-times-consequences approach to assess selected border threats.

Estimating the Likelihood of Border Threats

DHS defines likelihood as the "chance of something happening, whether defined, measured or estimated objectively or subjectively, or in terms of general descriptors (such as rare, unlikely, likely, almost certain), frequencies, or probabilities."[97] In general, there are two main approaches to estimating likelihood: based on observations of historical trends (past frequency), which may be used to calculate the probability that an event will occur, or based on analytic predictions about expected frequencies. Both approaches confront certain limits, however.

Likelihood as Past Frequency

How often a particular threat event has actually occurred within a given time period can be defined as its frequency. Over the long run, the frequency with which an event occurs may be used to estimate its probability, as scientists do, for example, in describing (based on previous observation) the probability that a category 5 hurricane will occur in a given year.[98]

For certain types of border threats, analysts may have historical data that allow them to describe such frequencies. In the case of unauthorized migration, for example, CBP and the legacy Immigration and Naturalization Service (INS) have used apprehensions of unauthorized migrants by the border patrol as a proxy to estimate unauthorized inflows.[99] Analysts also use U.S. Census data to estimate the stock of unauthorized migrants within the United States.[100] Apprehensions and survey data also may offer insight into illegal drug flows, in this case by analyzing drug seizures and data on the availability of illegal drugs within the United States.[101]

Yet deriving probabilities from historical observations is problematic. On a basic level, how exactly should illegal flows be counted? Historical frequencies may focus on illegal incidents— the number of illegal crossings— or on quantities, such as the number of individual migrants, or pounds (or tons) of illegal drugs or contraband. A given threat such as drug smuggling or illegal migration does not occur with equal frequency along all parts of the border, but varies between the Southwest versus the Northern and coastal borders, as well as among different portions of the Southwest border and by mode of entry (air, land, or sea).

More importantly, measures of past frequencies are only of *known* frequencies and not *actual* flows. For instance, while data from the National Seizure System indicate that over 1.7 million kilograms of illegal drugs were seized along the Southwest border in 2010,[102] this is not indicative of the total amount of illicit drugs smuggled across the Southwest border and into the United States for that time period. Estimates of successful illegal inflows—whether of illegal drugs, unauthorized migrants, or some other illicit flow—are just that: estimates. Learning from past history is even more problematic when it comes to rare events like attempted terrorist attacks. Probability models based on historical frequencies are poorly equipped to describe one-in-a-million chances, or to distinguish between, say, chances that are one-in-a-million versus one-in-a-billion or one-in-one-hundred-thousand.[103] Especially when combined with the fact that the stakes may be high, as in the case of terrorism, rare event probability models may not be sufficiently accurate to generate quantitative predictions about the probability of a future incident.[104] Partly for this reason, the intelligence community often describes likelihood in terms of qualitative ranges, such as "remote," "unlikely," "probable," etc.[105]

More generally, historical analysis is limited because "past performance is no guarantee of future results." Changes to the underlying model may invalidate long-term probabilities. Scientists use long-term frequencies to calculate the probability of severe weather, for example; but some people believe that rising temperatures and sea level may have altered climate dynamics so that probability models describing "500-year" floods and "100-year" storms may no longer be accurate. Similarly, some social scientists believe labor market and demographic changes in the United States and migration countries of origin, along with the decades-long escalation in U.S. enforcement, may have fundamentally altered regional immigration dynamics.

Likelihood as Expected Frequency

An argument can be made that historical frequency—how many terrorists traversed the U.S. border in 2010, for example—fails to capture the likelihood of certain border threats. Frequency only attempts to measure events that have occurred in the past. But how can the likelihood of a dreaded event such as the smuggling of WMD into the United States be evaluated if it has few precedents or is unprecedented? And even where a track record exists, as with unauthorized migration and illegal drugs and other contraband, what can be done to increase the accuracy of estimated probabilities?

The observations of past frequencies may be supplemented with analysis by subject field experts to make more informed predictions about the *expected* frequency of future events. With respect to the threat of terrorism, for example, federal law enforcement and intelligence analysts help estimate the likelihood of a terrorist attack. This involves many factors aside from historical frequency, such as probing and evaluating the motives of threat actors, their organizational structures, and their capabilities, as well as estimating the impact of broad social, political, or economic forces on these actors. Intelligence analysts and others may look at similar data to estimate the future likelihood of illegal drug flows and other contraband, and social scientists (as well as analysts) may examine market and social forces to model future migration flows. A key component in these processes is the development of indicators or milestones to warn of increased likelihood. For example, indicators may be used to evaluate whether a specific terrorist group is coming closer to realizing its plans to smuggle operatives into the United States. In such a scenario, milestones may include evidence of the group's efforts to recruit document forgers or specialists with experience smuggling people into the United States. One scholar has suggested that "Warning seeks to turn a mystery—'Are they going to attack?'—into a puzzle by identifying indicators along the path to war and then monitoring them."[106] Ideally, as indicators are met (or not), the chances of an attack are reevaluated and updated. Analysts use established analytical processes to gauge likelihood as new information rolls in about the targets they study.[107]

Yet models of illegal flows also are characterized by uncertainty, meaning that analysts never know precisely what data to look for. To be useful as a threat indicator, information must be valid relative to the threat being analyzed—that is, it must relate to the actual evolution of the threat. Indicators also should be reliably and consistently observable, and the earlier they are visible in the evolution of a threat, the more valuable they are to decision makers. Likewise, an indicator's persistence over time allows for its repeated measurement and reevaluation.[108] Finally, the more *visible* and the more *unique* indicators are, the easier it is to use them.

For example, the actual attainment of a particular milestone by a terrorist group—such as the successful recruitment of a document forger—may not be especially observable or *visible* to U.S. intelligence agencies. This makes it a poor indicator. In other words, effectively identifying a terrorist group's achievement of an indicator requires the capacity to witness it or obtain evidence of it. The more *unique* an indicator is, the easier it is to identify upon achievement. An indicator may be consistent with a number of activities, not just the one of interest to intelligence analysts. The recruitment of document forgers may not be a unique indication that a terrorist group will cross the U.S. border, for example. The forger may have been recruited to produce unrelated documents.[109]

The Strategic Actor Problem

Beyond these definitional and measurement problems, an additional obstacle to estimating the likelihood of particular border threats is that threat actors like unauthorized migrants, transnational criminal organizations, and potential terrorists are strategic and may adapt their behavior in response to U.S. border enforcement efforts. In this regard, risk models for border security differ in important ways from risk models for natural disasters, industrial failures, or financial investments, for example. The intelligent actor problem means that any effort to describe the likelihood of a given threat must account for given security conditions.[110] Any particular risk assessment can only represent a "snapshot" at a single point in time within a constantly evolving dynamic system. Some have suggested that intelligent actors cast doubt on the entire decision-theoretic risk assessment approach, and that DHS instead should rely on game theory, an approach which places greater emphasis on the preferences and strategic goals of terrorists and other threat actors.[111]

Evaluating Potential Consequences of Border Threats

Any given border threat may result in a range of potential consequences, and policymakers may disagree about how to evaluate them. The process of evaluating consequences includes at least three discrete tasks: defining the scope of a threat (i.e., the types of consequences), measuring the potential impact, and attaching value to the impact. Members of Congress may reach different conclusions about potential consequences at each stage of this evaluation process.

Defining Consequences

DHS defines consequence as "the effect of an incident, event, or occurrence, whether discreet or indirect."[112] The first step in evaluating the potential consequences of a given threat is to define its scope: what type of impact may occur? Many traditional risk assessment methodologies limit their analysis to concrete criteria, including in particular *direct economic costs* and *loss of life*.[113] An advantage to defining consequences narrowly in this way is that both of these criteria are relatively easy to quantify (i.e., in dollars and in the absolute number of lost lives), and analysts may make specific predictions about these potential impacts. An alternative approach considers a wider scope of consequences. In its Strategic National Risk Assessment, for example, DHS identifies six broad categories of potential consequences: *loss of life*, *injuries and illness*, *direct economic costs*, *social displacement*, *psychological distress*, and *environmental impact*.[114] An advantage to adopting this more expansive definition is that, for certain types of threats, these additional consequences may be at least as important as the economic and mortality effects.[115] On the other hand, psychological and sociological effects such as the impact of illegal migration on the rule of law, or the ways illegal drugs affect the families and communities of users, also may be far more difficult to define and quantify in a bounded or concrete fashion.

Measuring Consequences

Once the scope of consequences has been defined, a second challenge is how to measure the potential impact of a given threat. One aspect of the measurement challenge concerns how close in time a given consequence must be to be attributed to a particular security incident. Even when focused on the relatively narrow category of loss of life, for example, consider the following two scenarios:

- A terrorist is smuggled into the United States, creates and detonates a car bomb; an individual is killed in the blast.
- A drug trafficker smuggles cocaine into the United States; over several months, a client continually uses cocaine supplied by this trafficker and eventually overdoses and dies.

Some may argue that because the ultimate impact of both scenarios is the loss of a single life, they should be deemed to have the same consequence. Others may see that the consequences should be defined differently based on the immediacy of the outcome. (Both of these scenarios also may have other types of consequences, including economic impacts, injuries and illnesses, psychological effects, etc.) Similar measurement questions exist with respect to geographic bounds (how wide an area should be considered) and whether and how to estimate second- and third-degree effects of a given threat versus restricting the analysis to immediate impacts. For example, what are the economic consequences of a transnational retail crime network? Members of this network enter the United States and operate in a number of criminal capacities including as boosters and fences.[116] Retailers incur direct economic costs from the loss of the pilfered goods, and also may incur second-degree costs from security spending to prevent merchandise loss; and federal and state governments may suffer lost tax revenues. There may be third-degree costs if the criminal network sells the stolen products and uses the proceeds to further additional criminal operations. For instance, federal law enforcement has reputedly traced the illicit proceeds from the theft and resale of infant formula to terrorist organizations and insurgent groups, including Hamas and Hezbollah.[117] Are economic costs limited to the duped retailer, or do they also include the associated costs to public and private security agencies charged with investigating the crimes and related criminal activities?

Partly for these reasons, analysts disagree—often by wide margins—about the potential consequences of different types of threats. In the case of unauthorized migration, for example, even when the analysis is limited to the narrowest economic question of fiscal impact,[118] estimates of net effects vary by wide margins.[119] The measurement challenge may be substantially greater when it comes to the potential consequences of unknown future threats, which may affect a range of different categories, and for which some of the effects are far more difficult to quantify. Indeed, for certain issues, reasonable people may fundamentally disagree about the very nature of the consequences: should the growing prominence of Spanish and other languages in American schools be celebrated as a sign of increasing diversity, or feared as a threat to the primacy of English as a national language?

Valuing Consequences

How one evaluates potential consequences also depends on who is making the judgment. For example, a smuggler bringing counterfeit medication into the United States impacts a range of individuals from law enforcement officers charged with detecting and preventing the entry of illegal goods, to individuals consuming the counterfeit drugs, to the legitimate manufacturer. Consumers may place the greatest value on the potential health consequences of consuming the counterfeit product. Legitimate manufacturers may perceive the issue primarily in terms of the economic consequences of their lost sales revenues and reputational costs. The border-related security challenges the United States faces can be framed, in part, in terms of motive: some threats arise directly from individuals who wish us ill; others do not.[120] Terrorists targeting the United States seek to cause us harm, while drug traffickers exist primarily to derive profit. What is more "threatening": terrorists who intend to harm U.S. interests, or drug traffickers who intend to earn illicit profits but cause mayhem in the process? In the end, should motive enter into any calculation of consequence among border threats? Are the consequences of an incident greater when they represent the culmination of a concerted effort to attack the United States? Ultimately, how one defines the scope of a given threat (i.e., what categories of consequences are considered) and how one weights the various categories under consideration are *inherently subjective* considerations. There is no "correct" way to value the loss of a human life,[121] for example, or the destruction of a particular ecological habitat, or disregard for the rule of law.

Assessment of Selected Border Threats

This section illustrates how a framework relying upon the interplay of likelihood and potential consequences may be used to conceptualize the risks associated with selected border threats. For any given threat, there is incomplete and often-subjective information regarding likelihood and possible impacts. Take, for example, criminal networks smuggling illegal drugs into the United States:

- What is the likelihood that illegal drugs will be smuggled into the United States? Within the universe of illegal drugs available in the United States, some are domestically produced, and some are smuggled over the international borders. Of the subset of smuggled drugs, only an unknown proportion is identified and seized by U.S. officials; and attributing a particular smuggling incident to a criminal network involves additional uncertainty. As such, the *known frequency* of criminal networks smuggling drugs into the United States is an unknown portion of total smuggling incidents—itself a subset of all illegal drug flows. These data may be supplemented with additional model-based data and intelligence analysis to estimate *expected frequency,* but these methods involve further uncertainty and subjectivity.
- What are the consequences of illegal drugs being smuggled into the United States? Should the analysis focus exclusively on the loss of life related to criminal networks smuggling drugs into the United States, or also consider economic, social, psychological, and other

consequences? Even if the analysis is limited to loss of life, does it account for indirect deaths, such as those resulting from an addict's criminal activities to support his habit? Is the death of a smuggler who dies of dehydration in the desert evaluated differently than a user's death from an overdose, or the death of a bystander caught in the crossfire between rival drug gangs?

Despite these challenges, Table 1 presents broad conclusions about several generic border threats. While the likelihood of a given threat may be measured based on known or expected frequency, the table presents data only on known (historic) frequencies related to given threats. Similarly, though the range of potential consequences is vast, the table outlines available information only on financial costs and loss of life directly associated with certain threats. As such, this table does not provide comprehensive information for policy makers to utilize in evaluating the risk of threats, but rather illustrates how policymakers may make such an assessment.

Table 1. Selected Border Threats

Scenario	Likelihood (Known Frequency)	Potential Consequence (Financial Costs and Loss of Life)
Terrorists Smuggle WMD into U.S. to Commit a Violent Act of Terrorism	Since 9/11 there have been no publicly known instances, and there are many technical obstacles to obtaining and smuggling a WMD.[a]	The release of a lethal biological agent in an unprotected population could cause an untold number of deaths and economic costs exceeding $1 trillion dollars.[b] One estimate suggests that a 10 kiloton nuclear detonation at the Port of Long Beach, CA would kill 60,000 people in its immediate aftermath and cause damages estimated at more than $1 trillion dollars.[c]
Unarmed Terrorists Illegally Enter U.S. to Commit a Violent Act of Terrorism	Since 9/11, there are no publicly known instances.	In New York City, the 9/11 attack claimed 2,753 lives. It has been estimated to have caused $55 billion in destroyed and damaged property and shattered livelihoods in the city. The broader economic impacts likely ranged between $40 billion and $122 billion.[d]
Criminal Network Smuggles Illegal Drugs into the U.S.	The USBP made 18,074 drug seizures in FY2011.[g]	There are no data on drug trafficking-related deaths in the United States, though there are estimates for source countries. The overall annual economic impact of illegal drug use (including direct and certain indirect effects) has been estimated at $193 billion.[f]

Scenario	Likelihood (Known Frequency)	Potential Consequence (Financial Costs and Loss of Life)
		Some estimates indicate that drugs smuggled from Mexico into the United States generate between $18 billion and $39 billion in U.S. wholesale drug proceeds for the Colombian and Mexican drug traffickers annually.[g]
Criminal Network Smuggles Counterfeit Goods into the U.S.	CBP and ICE made 24,792 intellectual property rights seizures in FY2011 for an average of 68 seizures per day.[h]	The value of IPR violations seized by CBP was estimated to be $178 million in FY2011.[i] The value of IPR violations that exceed detection is unknown. Some counterfeit goods also may represent threats to U.S. health and safety, possibly resulting in lost lives.
Unauthorized Migrants Enter the U.S.	CBP made 340,252 apprehensions in FY2011[j]	Immigration affects the U.S. economy in complex ways, but on balance economic research suggests that the overall economic impact of unauthorized migration is "close enough to zero to be essentially a wash."[k] Available evidence suggests that criminality rates among legal and unauthorized aliens are about the same as, or possibly lower than, criminality rates in the total U.S. population[l] Hundreds of unauthorized migrants die each year while attempting to enter the United States.[m]

Sources: CRS analysis of publically available research, including sources cited below.

Notes: Table does not include an exhaustive accounting of potential consequences

[a] Archived CRS Report RL33787, *Maritime Security: Potential Terrorist Attacks and Protection Priorities*.

[b] *National Strategy for Countering Biological Threats,* November 2009, http://www.whitehouse.gov/sites/default/ files/National_Strategy_for_Countering_BioThreats.pdf.

[c] Charles Meade and Roger C. Molader, *Considering the Effects of a Catastrophic Terrorist Attack*, RAND Center for Terrorirsm Risk Management Policy, Santa Monica, CA, 2006, http://www.rand.org/pubs/ technical_reports/2006/RAND_ TR391.pdf.

[d] "The Reckoning: America and the World a Decade After 9/11." *New York Times*, September 8, 2011, http://www.nytimes.com/interactive/us/sept-11-reckoning /viewer.html.

[e] Customs and Border Protection, *On a Typical Day in Fiscal Year 2011*, March 7, 2012, http://cbp.gov/ linkhandler/cgov/about/accomplish/typical_ day_fy11. ctt/typical_day_fy11.pdf.

[f] U.S. Department of Justice, National Drug Intelligence Center (NDIC), *The Economic Impact of Illicit Drug Use on American Society*, Product No. 2011-Q0317-002,

May 2011. The NDIC estimate regards the *overall* economic impact of illegal drug use, including both drugs imported into the United States and drugs produced domestically.

[g] U.S. Department of Justice, National Drug Intelligence Center, *National Drug Threat Assessment 2009*, Product No. 2008-Q0317-005, December 2008. According to ONDCP data, the trafficking and distribution of cocaine generates about $3.9 billion, marijuana generates about $8.5 billion, and methamphetamine generates about $1 billion. Jane's, *Security, Mexico*, February 20, 2009.

[h] Customs and Border Protection, *On a Typical Day in Fiscal Year 2011*, March 7, 2012,.

[i] Customs and Border Protection *Intellectual Property Rights Fiscal Year 2011 Seizure Statistics,* http://www.cbp.gov/linkhandler/cgov/trade/priority_trade /ipr/ipr_communications/seizure/ ipr_seizures_fy2011.ctt/ipr_seizure_fy2011.pdf.

[j] U.S. Border Patrol, "Apprehensions/Seizure Statistics—Fiscal Year 2011,".

[k] Gordon Hanson, "The Economics and Policy of Illegal Immigration in the United States," Migration Policy Institute, Washington, DC, December 2009,.

[l] CRS Report R42057, *Interior Immigration Enforcement: Programs Targeting Criminal Aliens.*

[m] CRS Report R42138, *Border Security: Immigration Enforcement Between Ports of Entry.*

CONCLUDING COMMENTS: POLICYMAKING CHALLENGES

Understanding the nuanced security issues posed by the flow of people and goods across U.S. borders is fundamental to shaping effective policy in this area. This report describes a possible framework for describing the risks posed by specific hazards at the border based on their likelihood and their potential consequences. While such an analysis may seem simple, its execution is complex, as described above, and *there is no objectively correct way to evaluate the relative importance of any particular threat at U.S. borders*. Nonetheless, the complexity and subjectivity of threat assessment does not diminish the importance of some form of threat assessment—explicit or otherwise—as a logical starting point for the policymaking process.

Beyond the challenges of threat assessment, how border *threats* shape border security *policies* also depends on a pair of mediating issues, as illustrated in Figure 4. First, while the border is a critical nexus for transnational flows, the *strategic breadth* of border threats and of policy responses extends well beyond the border region. At the very least, this suggests the importance of understanding how border-specific policy proposals may impact other government initiatives or interests, and how other law enforcement activities may supplement efforts at the border.

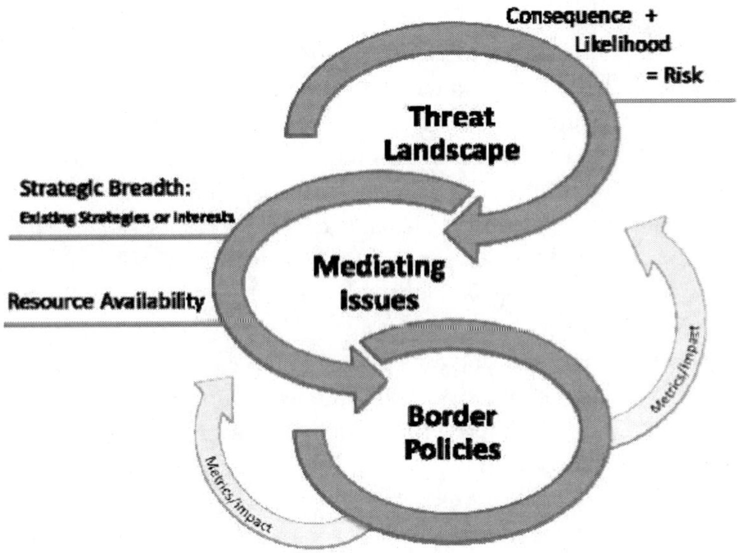

Source: CRS analysis.

Figure 4. Border Policymaking Context.

For example, lawmakers concerned about illegal drug flows through the ports of entry may favor increased investments in specific DHS equities such as port of entry infrastructure, more CBP officers, non-intrusive inspection scanners, and drug sniffing dogs. For Members focused on counterterrorism, priorities might include continued investments in DHS information systems, such as the CBP Automated Targeting System, the U.S. Visitor and Immigrant Status Indicator Technology (US-VISIT) system,[122] and the Automated Commercial Environment, along with investments in intelligence collection programs to ensure that the right data are being analyzed. Yet such investments compete with other border priorities, such as fencing and surveillance equipment between ports.

Border investments also complement and interact with law enforcement activities beyond the border, such as—in the case of illegal drugs—programs to combat traffickers' money laundering schemes and to detect and prevent southbound flows of money and guns. Some of the most important work with respect to counterterrorism and counternarcotics efforts may involve bilateral and multilateral partnerships with allies abroad. And the U.S. government has vital competing interests in facilitating effective commercial flows and the efficient movement of legal travelers. Inevitably, decisions about "border security" must grapple with the full universe of threats and policies that intersect at U.S. borders.

Second, the *availability of resources* also plays a role in framing border security policy. Immediately after the 9/11 attacks, the convergence of immigration control, the war on drugs, and the urgency attached to combating terrorism meant that DHS took more of an "all of the above" approach to border security. Yet even when budgets are expanding, Congress and DHS face tradeoffs among the different elements of DHS's border security mission. As budgeting has grown tighter in the current fiscal climate, policymakers face increasingly difficult questions about how to set priorities and where to allocate scarce resources.

The answers, in turn, depend on a third set of questions concerning how to measure and evaluate the effectiveness of border security policies. What does a secure border mean in real terms? How do we measure progress toward this goal? The Secure Fence Act (P.L. 109-367) defines operational control of the border to mean *zero illegal inflows*,[123] yet many analysts doubt that an open country in a globalized economy can ever achieve a 100% interdiction rate—and some question whether such a standard is even worth aspiring to.[124]

Clearly articulated and attainable policy goals help in the development of effective metrics and appropriate benchmarks. How to measure the success of policies designed to curb unauthorized migration may be especially important—and challenging—during a period experiencing net unauthorized migration flows at around zero. Two key measurement-related questions are how recent DHS policies like increased border personnel, CBP's consequence delivery system, and ICE's Secure Communities[125] program have contributed to the recent trend of falling illegal inflows;[126] and the degree to which unauthorized flows will increase as the U.S. economy recovers and new hiring resumes.

Surveying the border policymaking context as described in Figure 1, Members of Congress may ask whether the U.S. approach to particular threats is too narrow or perhaps too broad. For example, should policy be designed to prevent *all* forms of unauthorized migration and illegal movement of goods, or should policies be tailored to target specific threats such as terrorists, transnational gangs, or illegal drugs?[127] If the answer lies somewhere between—involving both sweeping and targeted programs—how should mediating issues such as resource allocation and the prioritization of one effort over another be weighed?

Finally, in addition to setting overall priorities, Members of Congress may evaluate policies by asking where DHS may get the most effective return on its enforcement investments. In addition to terrorism prevention, some Members may emphasize investments in resiliency, or the ability to survive and manage a terrorist attack. Members concerned with preventing the inflow of illegal drugs may question whether the enforcement component of overall U.S. drug policy is properly balanced with non-enforcement investments. Members focused on countering the movement of bulk cash, counterfeit goods, and other smuggled items across the U.S. borders may weigh the value of investing in enforcement personnel at the border, versus focusing on international cooperation and domestic intelligence collection and information.

End Notes

[1] U.S. Customs and Border Protection (CBP), "CBPs 2011 Fiscal Year in Review," December 12, 2011. Cargo flows through U.S. ports (imports plus exports) was valued at $3.7 trillion in 2011, about 25% of U.S. gross domestic product (GDP); and international tourism to the United States (exports) was valued at $134 billion in 2010, about 1% of GDP; see CRS Report RL33577, *U.S. International Trade: Trends and Forecasts*, by Brock R. Williams and J. Michael Donnelly; and CRS Report R41409, *U.S. Travel and Tourism Industry*, by Suzanne M. Kirchhoff.

[2] CBP, "CBPs 2011 Fiscal Year in Review," December 12, 2011.

[3] Jeffrey Passel and D.Vera Cohn, *Unauthorized Immigrants: 11.1 Million in 2011*, Pew Research Hispanic Center, Washington, DC, December 6, 2012, http://www. pewhispanic.org /2012/12/06/unauthorized-immigrants-11-1-millionin-2011/.

[4] U.S. Department of Justice, National Drug Intelligence Center, *National Drug Threat Assessment 2011*, http://www.justice.gov/ndic/pubs44/44849/44849p.pdf.

[5] Department of Justice, Department of Health and Human Services, Department of State, Department of Labor, Department of Homeland Security, and U.S. Agency of International Development, Assessment of U.S. Government Efforts to Combat Trafficking in Persons, June 2004. Subsequent Justice Department reports have cited this 2004 figure, or not included estimates of the number of trafficking victims. For a fuller discussion see CRS Report RL34317, *Trafficking in Persons: U.S. Policy and Issues for Congress*, by Alison Siskin and Liana Sun Wyler.

[6] Department of Homeland Security (DHS), *Quadrennial Homeland Security Review Report: A Strategic Framework for a Secure Homeland*, Washington, DC, February 2010, page 26; hereafter: DHS, *QHSR*.

[7] See U.S. Congress, House Committee on Homeland Security, *The Department of Homeland Security: An Assessment of the Department and a Roadmap for its Future*, 112th Cong., 2nd sess., September 20, 2012.

[8] DHS, *Risk Management Fundamentals: Homeland Security Risk Management Doctrine*, Washington, DC, April 2011 (hereafter: DHS, *Risk Management Doctrine*), page 7.

[9] As the *Quadrennial Homeland Security Review* observes, "because the term is in such widespread use, it may be easy today to overlook the fact that *homeland security* is a relatively new concept." The QHSR defines homeland security as "the intersection of evolving threats and hazards with the traditional governmental and civic responsibilities of civil defense, emergency response, law enforcement, customs, border control, and immigration" (DHS, *QHSR*, p. 11).

[10] The Aliens Act of June 25, 1798 (1 Statutes-at-Large 570), and the Alien Enemy Act of July 6, 1798 (1 Statutes-atLarge 577), respectively. Three laws passed prior to June 1798 concerned federal naturalization provisions.

[11] Respectively, the Immigration Act of March 3, 1903 (32 Statutes-at-Large 1213); the Act of May 22, 1918 (40 Statutes-at-Large 559); the Internal Security Act of 1950 (64 Statutes-at-large 987); the Immigration Act of 1990 (P.L. 101-649).

[12] See U.S. Customs and Border Protection (CBP), "Border Patrol History," http://www.cbp.gov/xp/cgov/ border_security/border_patrol/border_patrol_ohs/history.xml. Also see Tony Payan, *The Three U.S.-Mexico Border Wars: Drugs, Immigration, and Homeland Security* (Westport, CT: Praeger Security International, 2006).

[13] Partly as a result of economic changes in the United States and Mexico, as well as the unintended consequences of changes to U.S. immigration policy during this period, the estimated number of unauthorized aliens in the United States increased sharply beginning in the late 1960s; see CRS Report R42560, *Mexican Migration to the United States: Policy and Trends*, coordinated by Marc R. Rosenblum.

[14] Timothy J. Dunn, *The Militarization of the U.S.-Mexico Border, 1978-1992: Low-Intensity Conflict Doctrine Comes Home* (Austin: CMA Books, University of Texas, 1996).

[15] Calculations from data available at CRS Report R42138, *Border Security: Immigration Enforcement Between Ports of Entry*, by Marc R. Rosenblum; and Syracuse University Transactional Records Access Clearinghouse, "National Trends in Apprehensions and Staffing," http://trac.syr.edu/immigration/reports/141/include/rep141table2.html.

[16] Calculations from data available at Department of Justice, "Drug Enforcement Administration," http://www.justice.gov/archive/jmd/1975_2002/2002/html/page100-103.htm; and CRS Report R42440, *Commerce, Justice, Science, and Related Agencies: FY2013 Appropriations*, coordinated by Nathan James, Jennifer D. Williams, and John F. Sargent Jr.

[17] P.L. 107-296, §402.

[18] On public health and border security, see CRS Report R40570, *Immigration Policies and Issues on Health-Related Grounds for Exclusion*, by Ruth Ellen Wasem.

[19] CRS Report RL33874, *Unauthorized Aliens Residing in the United States: Estimates Since 1986*, by Ruth Ellen Wasem.

[20] See U.S. Department of Justice, National Drug Intelligence Center, *National Drug Threat Assessment 2011*, pp. 13- 16, http://www.justice.gov/ndic/pubs44/44849/44849p.pdf.

[21] Thus, this report does not focus on other types of transnational threats, including cybercrimes and the theft of U.S. intellectual property through electronic means, neither of which is geographically connected to U.S. borders, or traditional threats associated with foreign militaries or international espionage, neither of which is primarily a DHS responsibility.

[22] Immigration and Nationality Act (INA) §212(a)(3)(B)(i); 8 U.S.C. 1182(a)(3)(B)(i). Under this definition, aliens who *intend to* engage in terrorist activities (i.e., *potential* terrorists) are prohibited from entering the United States. Also see CRS Report RL32564, *Immigration: Terrorist Grounds for Exclusion and Removal of Aliens*, by Michael John Garcia and Ruth Ellen Wasem.

[23] For a fuller discussion of terrorism and international crime, also see CRS Report R41004, *Terrorism and Transnational Crime: Foreign Policy Issues for Congress*, by John Rollins and Liana Sun Wyler.

[24] Anthony F. Lemieux and Victor H. Asal, "Grievance, Social Dominance Orientation, and Authoritarianism in the Choice and Justification of Terror Versus Protest," *Dynamics of Asymmetric Conflict,* vol. 3, no. 3, (November 2010), p. 196. See also: Ryan Hunter and Danielle Heinke, "Radicalization of Islamist Terrorists in the Western World," *FBI Law Enforcement Bulletin,* (September 2011), pp. 27-29, http://www.fbi.gov/stats-services/publications/lawenforcement-bulletin/september-2011. Hunter and Heinke rely on the ideas of scholar Peter Neumann. Hereafter: Hunter and Heinke, "Radicalization of Islamist."

[25] Louise Richardson, *What Terrorists Want: Understanding the Enemy, Containing the Threat* (New York: Random House, 2007), p. 16. Hereafter: Richardson, *What Terrorists Want.* Marc Sageman has suggested that Muslim terrorists are—in part—inspired by a sense of moral outrage. Marc Sageman, *Leaderless Jihad: Terror Networks in the Twenty-First Century,* (Philadelphia: University of Pennsylvania Press, 2008), pp. 72 75.

[26] Hunter and Heinke, "Radicalization of Islamist"; also see Ervin Staub, "Understanding and Responding to Group Violence: Genocide, Mass Killing, and Terrorism," in *Understanding Terrorism: Psychosocial Roots, Consequences, and Interventions*, ed. Fathali M. Moghaddam and Anthony J. Marsella (Washington, DC: American Psychological Association, 2004).

[27] Richardson, *What Terrorists Want,* p. 13.

[28] INA §212(a)(3)(B)(iii); 8 U.S.C. 1182(a)(3)(B)(iii).

[29] Thomas F. Ditzler, "Malevolent Minds: The Teleology of Terrorism," in *Understanding Terrorism: Psychosocial Roots, Consequences, and Interventions*, ed. Fathali M. Moghaddam and Anthony J. Marsella (Washington, DC: American Psychological Association, 2004), p 197.

[30] Robert A. Pape, *Dying to Win: The Strategic Logic of Suicide Terrorism* (New York: Random House, 2005), pp. 9- 10.

[31] "Moral turpitude" has been a basis for exclusion since 1891, and its meaning has been determined by judicial and administrative case law, rather than by statute. In general, crimes involve moral turpitude if they manifest an element of baseness or depravity under current mores. See CRS Report RL32480, *Immigration Consequences of Criminal Activity*, by Michael John Garcia.

[32] INA §212(a)(2); U.S.C. §1182(a)(2). Also see ibid.

[33] This distinction does not preclude cooperation between criminals and terrorists. Frank E. Hagan, "'Organized Crime' and 'organized crime' Indeterminate Problems of Definition," *Trends in Organized Crime,* vol. 9, no. 4 (Summer 2006), p. 135. See also James O. Finkenauer, "Problems of Definition: What Is Organized Crime?" *Trends in Organized Crime,* vol. 8, no. 3 (Spring 2005), pp. 65. Hereafter Finkenauer, "Problems of Definition."

[34] Diego d'Andria, "Investment Strategies of Criminal Organisations," *Policy Studies,* vol. 32, no. 1 (January 2011), p. 3.

[35] Federal Bureau of Investigation, "The MS-13 Threat: A National Assessment," January 14, 2008, http://www.fbi.gov/news/stories/2008/january/ms13_011408. Also see Virginia Fusion Center, Mara Salvatrucha 13 (MS-13) Intelligence Report, (Commonwealth of Virginia Department of State Police: July 2008), pp. 8-9.

[36] Klaus von Lampe, "Re-Conceptualizing Transnational Organized Crime: Offenders as Problem Solvers," *International Journal of Security and Terrorism*, vol. 2, no. 1 (2011), p. 11. Hereafter: von Lampe, "Re-Conceptualizing."

[37] Finkenauer, "Problems of Definition," p. 67.

[38] Toine Spapens, "Macro Networks, Collectives, and Business Processes: An Integrated Approach to Organized Crime," *European Journal of Crime, Criminal Law, and Criminal Justice*, vol. 18 (2010), pp. 210-212.

[39] See Pen Wang, "The Crime-Terror Nexus: Transformation, Alliance, Convergence," *Asian Social Science,* vol. 6, no. 6 (2010), p. 13; also see Finkenauer, "Problems of Definition."

[40] See for example, Phil Williams, "The Terrorism Debate Over Mexican Drug Trafficking Violence," *Terrorism and Political Violence,* vol. 24, no. 1, (April 2012).

[41] See Moisés Naím, "Mafia States: Organized Crime Takes Office," *Foreign Affairs*, vol. 91, no. 3, (May/Jun2012), pp. 100-111.

[42] INA §§212(a)(1)-(7); 8 U.S.C. §§1227 (a)(1)-(7).

[43] See for example, Elizabeth Fussell, "Space, Time, and Volition: Dimensions of Migration Theory," in *Oxford Handbook of International Migration*, ed. Marc R. Rosenblum and Daniel J. Tichenor (New York, NY: Oxford University Press, 2012), pp. 25-52.

[44] About one-half to two-thirds of unauthorized migrants are believed to enter the United States illegally, either by evading inspection or using fraudulent documents; the remaining one-third to one-half enter legally on a nonimmigrant visa but fail to depart and/or otherwise violate the terms of their visa. See CRS Report RS22446, *Nonimmigrant Overstays: Brief Synthesis of the Issue*, by Ruth Ellen Wasem.

[45] Unlawful presence in the United States absent additional factors is a civil violation, not a criminal offense; see CRS Report RL32480, *Immigration Consequences of Criminal Activity*, by Michael John Garcia. Research by CRS and other analysts suggest that criminality rates among the foreign-born (i.e., including legal and unauthorized migrants) likely is no more than—and possibly is below—rates among the native born; see CRS Report R42057, *Interior Immigration Enforcement: Programs Targeting Criminal Aliens*, by Marc R. Rosenblum and William A. Kandel. Also see for example, Lesley Williams Reid, Harald E. Weiss, and Robert M. Adelman, et al., "The Immigration-Crime Relationship: Evidence Across U.S. Metropolitan Areas," *Social Science Research*, Vol. 34, no. 4 (December 2005: pp. 757-780.

[46] Immigration-related identity and document fraud are believed to be widespread, but reliable estimates of their pervasiveness are not available. See archived CRS Report RL34007, *Immigration Fraud: Policies, Investigations, and Issues*, by Ruth Ellen Wasem. On the links between Mexican drug trafficking organizations and human smuggling groups, also see U.S. Office of National Drug Control Policy, *National Southwest Border Counternarcotics Strategy*, http://www.whitehouse.gov/sites/default/files/ondcp/policy-and-research/swb_counternarcotics_strategy11.pdf, p. 17.

[47] Department of Homeland Security, *Quadrennial Homeland Security Review Report: A Strategic Framework for a Secure Homeland*, February 2010, p. 6, http://www.dhs.gov /xlibrary/assets/qhsr_report.pdf.

[48] Federal Bureau of Investigation, *Weapons of Mass Destruction: Frequently Asked Questions*, http://www.fbi.gov/about-us/investigate/terrorism/wmd/wmd_faqs.

[49] Phil Williams, "Terrorism, Organized Crime, and WMD Smuggling: Challenge and Response," *Strategic Insights*, vol. VI, no. 5 (August 2007).

[50] For more information on gun trafficking, specifically along the Southwest border, see CRS Report R40733, *Gun Trafficking and the Southwest Border*, by Vivian S. Chu and William J. Krouse; and CRS Report RL32842, *Gun Control Legislation*, by William J. Krouse.

[51] See for example, David A. Shirk, *The Drug War in Mexico: Confronting a Shared Threat*, Council on Foreign Relations, Council Special Report No. 60, Washington, DC, March 2011, p. 13.

[52] Customs and Border Protection, *On a Typical Day in Fiscal Year 2011*, March 7, 2012, http://cbp.gov/linkhandler/ cgov/about/accomplish/typical_day_fy11.ctt/typical_day_fy11.pdf.

[53] For information on U.S. intellectual property rights laws and related issues, see CRS Report RL34292, *Intellectual Property Rights and International Trade*, by Shayerah Ilias and Ian F. Fergusson.

[54] U.S. Customs and Border Protection, *Intellectual Property Rights Fact Sheet*, http://www.cbp.gov/linkhandler/cgov/ newsroom/fact_sheets/trade/ipr_fact_sheet.ctt/ipr_fact_sheet.pdf.

[55] According to U.S. Customs and Border Protection, "domestic value" is the "cost of seized goods, plus the cost of shipping and importing the goods into the U.S. and an amount for profit."

[56] U.S. Customs and Border Protection, *IPR Seizure Statistics*, http://www.cbp.gov/xp /cgov/trade/priority_trade/ipr/ ipr_communications/seizure/.

[57] Michigan Liquor Control Commission, *Illegal Importation of Alcohol Into Michigan: An Assessment of the Issue and Recommendations*, Legislative Committee Report, January 15, 2008, http://www.michigan.gov/documents/dleg/ Illegal_Importation_of_Alcohol_1_ 14_08_221682_7.pdf. It is unclear how much of this smuggling is international and how much is interstate. Smuggling alcohol *out* of the United States by criminal networks also results in revenues losses for governments in Europe, Russia, Asia, and the Western Hemisphere; see Interagency Working Group, *International Crime Threat Assessment*, Pursuant to the President's International Crime Control Strategy, December 2000.

[58] U.S. Government Accountability Office, *Illicit Tobacco: Various Schemes are Used to Evade Taxes and Fees*, GAO-11-313, March 2011, p. 6, http://www.gao.gov/new.items /d11313.pdf.

[59] International Tax and Investment Center, *The Illicit Trade in Tobacco Products and How to Tackle It*, http://www.kangaroogroup.eu/DB_beelden/booklet_illicit_trade _tobacco_ products.pdf. Bureau of Alcohol, Tobacco, Firearms, and Explosives, *Cigarette Smuggling Linked to Terrorism*, June 18, 2004, http://www.atf.gov/pub/gen_pub/ cigarette smuggling.pdf.

[60] Bulk cash smuggling is described under 31 U.S.C. §5332 as "knowingly conceal[ing] more than $10,000 in currency or other monetary instruments on the person ... or in any conveyance, article of luggage, merchandise, or other container, and transport[ing] or transfer[ing] or attempt[ing] to transport or transfer such currency or monetary instruments from a place within the United States to a place outside of the United States, or from a place outside the United States to a place within the United States" with intent to evade currency reporting requirements. Taking $10,000 or more out of the United States is not considered illegal, so long as it is declared and reported. See 31 C.F.R. §103.23(a).

[61] Office of National Drug Control Strategy, *National Southwest Border Counternarcotics Strategy*, June 2009, p. 25, http://www.whitehousedrugpolicy.gov/publications/swb_ counternarcotics_strategy09/ swb_counternarcotics_strategy09.pdf.

[62] William Booth and Nick Miroff, "Stepped-Up Efforts by U.S., Mexico Fail to Stem Flow of Drug Money South," *Washington Post,* August 25, 2010, http://www.washingtonpost.com /wp-dyn/content/article/2010/08/25/ AR2010082506161.html.

[63] Customs and Border Protection, *On a Typical Day in Fiscal Year 2011*, March 7, 2012, http://cbp.gov/linkhandler/ cgov/about/accomplish/typical_day_fy11.ctt /typical_day_fy11. pdf.

[64] For an introduction to risk assessment and probabilistic risk assessment, see for example Mark Jablonowski , *Precautionary Risk Management: Dealing with Catastrophic Loss Potentials in Business, the Community and Society* (New York: Palgrave, 2006); herafter: Jablonowski, *Precautionary Risk Management.* Also see Hiromitsu Kumamoto, *Satisfying Safety Goals by Probabilistic Risk Assessment* (London: Springer, 2007); Barry Charles Ezell, Steven P. Bennett, and Detloff von Winterfeldt, et al., "Probabilistic Risk Analysis and Terrorism Risk," *Risk Analysis*, vol. 30, no. 4 (2010); hereafter: Ezell et al., "Probabilistic Risk Analysis."

[65] See for example, DHS, "Homeland Security Secretary Michael Chertoff Announces Six-Point Agenda for Department of Homeland Security," Press Release, July 13, 2005. For a fuller discussion of DHS's approach to risk management, see archived CRS Report RL33858, *The Department of Homeland Security's Risk Assessment Methodology: Evolution, Issues, and Options for Congress*, by Todd Masse, Siobhan O'Neil, and John Rollins.

[66] See archived CRS Report RL33858, *The Department of Homeland Security's Risk Assessment Methodology: Evolution, Issues, and Options for Congress*, by Todd Masse, Siobhan O'Neil, and John Rollins.

[67] DHS, "Fact Sheet: FY2012 Homeland Security Grant Program," http://www.fema.gov/library /viewRecord.do? fromSearch=fromsearch&id=6184. About 19% of State Homeland Security Program funds are distributed based on minimum amounts guaranteed to states and territories, with the remainder distributed based on risk and anticipated effectiveness.

[68] See DHS, "Privacy Impact Assessment Update for the Automated Targeting System," Washington, DC, December 2, 2008, http://foia.cbp.gov/streamingWord.asp?i=41. All travelers and cargo entering the United States are subject to primary inspection, when CBP officers at ports of entry make a basic admissibility determination. Secondary inspection refers to a more extensive inspection process that may include a scan and/or physical examination of cargo and additional questioning and/or a search of a traveler's vehicle, possessions, or person, among other forms of scrutiny. CBP officers may subject travelers and cargo to secondary inspection regardless of their ATS risk scores.

[69] The White House, *Homeland Security Presidential Directive (HSPD) 10: Biodefense for the 21st Century*, Washington, DC, 2004; the White House, *HSPD 18: Medical Countermeasures Against Weapons of Mass Destruction*, Washington, DC, 2007; the White House, *HSPD 22: National Domestic Chemical Defense*, Washington, DC, 2008.

[70] Event trees are a type of logic tree using nodes and branches to model a sequence of uncertain events that may lead to consequences; probabilities (or probability distributions) are attached to each branch at each node, and downstream outcomes are calculated by multiplying the probabilities along a given branch. See Ezell et al., "Probabilistic Risk Analysis."

[71] See testimony by Segaran Pillai, Chief Medical and Science Advisor DHS Science and Technology Directorate Chemical and Biological Defense Division, before the U.S. Congress, House Committee on Homeland Security, Subcommittee on Emergency Preparedness, Response, and Communications, *Taking Measure of Countermeasures (Part I)*, 112th Cong., 1st sess., April 14, 2011; hereafter: Pillai testimony.

[72] See U.S. Government Accountability Office, *National Preparedness: DHS and HHS Can Further Strengthen Coordination for Chemical, Biological, Radiological, and Nuclear Risk Assessments*, GAO-11-606, June 2011, http://www.gao.gov/new.items/d11606.pdf.

[73] The White House, *Presidential Policy Directive (PPD) 8: National Preparedness*, Washington, DC, March 30, 2011.

[74] DHS, "The Strategic National Risk Assessment in Support of PPD 8: A Comprehensive Risk-Based Approach toward a Secure and Resilient Nation," Washington, DC, December 2011; hereafter: DHS, SNRA 2011.

[75] Ibid., p. 2.

[76] DHS, *QHSR*.

[77] Ibid., pp. 6-8. The QHSR identifies five core homeland security missions: preventing terrorism and enhancing security, securing and managing our borders, enforcing and administering our immigration laws, safeguarding and securing cyberspace, and ensuring resilience to disasters.

[78] CBP, *Secure Borders, Safe Travel, Legal Trade: U.S. Customs and Border Protection Fiscal Year 2009-2014 Strategic Plan*, Washington, DC: 2009 (Hereinafter CBP, *2009 Strategic Plan*), p. 5.

[79] Ibid., p. 11.

[80] USBP 2004 Strategic Plan

[81] USBP 2012-16 strategic plan, p. 7. Also see testimony by Michael Fisher, Chief, U.S. Customs and Border Protection Office of Border Patrol, before the House Homeland Security Committee, Subcommittee on Border and Maritime Security, *Measuring Border Security: U.S. Border patrol's New Strategic Plan and the Path Forward*, 112th Congress, 2nd sess., May 8, 2012.

[82] DHS Risk Steering Committee, *DHS Risk Lexicon 2010 Edition*, Washington, DC, September 2010; hereafter: DHS, *Risk Lexicon.*

[83] DHS, *Risk Management Fundamentals: Homeland Security Risk Management Doctrine*, Washington, DC, April 2011; hereafter: DHS, *Risk Management Fundamentals.*

[84] DHS, *Risk Lexicon*, p. vii.

[85] Ibid., p. 5.

[86] Ibid., pp. 15-26. Also see Jablonowski, *Precautionary Risk Management*, p. 64; National Research Council, Committee on Methodological Improvements to the Department of Homeland Security's Biological Agent Risk Analysis, *Department of Homeland Security Bioterrorism Risk Assessment: A Call for Change* (Washington, DC: National Academies Press, 2008); hereafter: NRC, *DHS Risk Assessment.*

[87] Sven Ove Hansson, "From the Casino to the Jungle: Dealing with Uncertainty in Technological Risk Management," *Synthese*, no. 168 (2009).

[88] See archived CRS Report RL33858, *The Department of Homeland Security's Risk Assessment Methodology: Evolution, Issues, and Options for Congress*, by Todd Masse, Siobhan O'Neil, and John Rollins. The DHS *Risk Management Fundamentals*, however, warns that including a separate measure of vulnerability "is sometimes not the best approach for ... homeland security risk assessments" in part "because interdependencies between the three variables, and/or poorly executed mathematical operations, can lead to inaccurate results." DHS, *Risk Management Fundamentals*, pp. 20-21. Also see Ezell, et al. "Probabilistic Risk Analysis." Although the HSGP nominally began using the so-called threat, vulnerability, consequences (TVC) framework in 2007, all areas and assets initially were assigned a vulnerability score of 1; and FY2011 was the first year in which vulnerability and

consequences were calculated separately. See DHS, *HSGP Guidance and Application Kit, FY2011*, Washington, DC, May 2011, p. 3.

89 See Pillai testimony; also see Sara Clucking, "DHS S&T Bioterrorism Risk Assessment (BTRA)," *International Symposium on Bioterrorism Risk*, October 6, 2009, http://www.biosecurity.sandia.gov/ibtr/subpages/pastConf/ 20082009/albuquerque/6dhs3.pdf.

90 DHS, *SNRA* 2011, p. 5.

91 For example, while DHS has published risk assessment methodologies for the HSGP programs related to terrorism and natural disasters, the department has not published a similar formula for Operation Stonegarden, which addresses illegal migration and border crime. Similarly, the Strategic National Risk Assessment explicitly excludes immigration and drugs from its analysis. And in their recent national strategy documents, CBP and USBP do not include descriptions of their risk assessment methodologies.

92 See for example, the White House, "Fixing the Immigration System for America's 21st Century Economy," http://www.whitehouse.gov/issues/fixing-immigration-system-america-s-21st-century-economy.

93 See for example, House Homeland Security Committee, Subcommittee on Border and Maritime Security, *Measuring Border Security: U.S. Border patrol's New Strategic Plan and the Path Forward*, 112th Congress, 2nd sess., May 8, 2012; U.S. Congress, House Committee on Homeland Security, *Secure Border Act of 2012*, report to accompany H.R. 1299, 112th Cong., 2nd sess., June 4, 2012.

94 See for example in the 112th Congress, the Department of Homeland Security Authorization Act of 2011 (S. 1546).

95 NRC, *DHS Risk Assessment.* Also see Ezell et al., "Probabilistic Risk Analysis."

96 Ibid.

97 DHS, *Risk Lexicon*, p. 20.

98 Ibid., p. 16.

99 See for example, National Research Council, Panel on Survey Options for Estimating the Flow of Unauthorized Crossings at the U.S.-Mexico Border, *Options for Estimating Illegal Entries at the U.S.-Mexico Border* (Washington, DC: National Academies Press, 2012)..

100 Ibid.

101 See for example, U.S. Department of Justice, National Drug Intelligence Center, *National Drug Threat Assessment 2011*, pp. 13-16, http://www.justice.gov/ndic/pubs44 /44849 /44849p.pdf.

102 These data were provided to CRS by the National Drug Intelligence Center. Data cover seizures of cocaine, heroin, marijuana, MDMA, and methamphetamine.

103 See Jablonowski, *Precautionary Risk Management.*

104 Ibid.

105 See for example DHS, *Risk Lexicon*, p. 20.

106 See Gregory F. Treverton, *Intelligence for an Age of Terror* (Cambridge: Cambridge University Press, 2009), pp. 39-40. Hereafter: Treverton, *Intelligence.* On indicators, also see U.S. Government, "A Tradecraft Primer: Structured Analytic Techniques for Improving Intelligence Analysis," March 2009, p. 12.

107 This form of analysis is consistent with DHS's statistical definition of likelihood as the "conditional probability of observing a particular event given [that a] hypothesis under consideration is true"; see DHS, *Risk Lexicon*, p. 20. In DHS's example, analysts may draw on a theoretical model of the relationship between border infrastructure, unauthorized

migration, and demographic trends to estimate the likelihood that a border fence has been breached based on their observation that the population of cities in the area has increased.

108 Richards J. Heuer, Jr. and Randolph H. Pherson, *Structured Analytic Techniques for Intelligence Analysis* (Washington, DC: CQ Press, 2011), p. 136.

109 Treverton, *Intelligence,* pp. 42-45. The indicators described above are predictive and are typically used in intelligence analysis. Law enforcement often also uses backward-looking descriptive indicators "to assess whether a target's ... behavior is consistent with an established pattern." See Heuer and Pherson, *Structured Analytic Techniques,* p. 132.

110 Thus, it may not be useful to distinguish between "threat" and "vulnerability" in these cases.

111 NRC, *DHS Risk Assessment*; Ezell et al., "Probabilistic Risk Analysis." A decision theoretic approach to risk assessment may account for strategic adversaries, at least to a degree, by developing sophisticated expected frequency models of threat scenarios.

112 DHS, *Risk Lexicon*, p. 10.

113 See for example, Charles Meade and Roger C. Molader, *Considering the Effects of a Catastrophic Terrorist Attack*, RAND Center for Terrorism Risk Management Policy, Santa Monica, CA, 2006, http://www.rand.org/pubs/ technical_reports/2006/RAND_TR391.pdf; also see see Sara Clucking, "DHS S&T Bioterrorism Risk Assessment (BTRA)," *International Symposium on Bioterrorism Risk*, October 6, 2009, http://www.biosecurity. sandia.gov/ibtr/ subpages/pastConf/20082009 /albuquerque/6dhs3. pdf.

114 Department of Homeland Security, *The Strategic National Risk Assessment in Support of PPD 8: A Comprehensive Risk-Based Approach Toward a Secure and Resilient Nation*, December 2011, p. 5, http://www.dhs.gov/xlibrary/assets/ rma-strategic-national-risk-assessment-ppd8.pdf.

115 Indeed, terrorists may design certain attacks specifically to instill fear in the target population, highlighting the importance of considering the psychological consequences of such a threat.

116 A "booster" is someone who steals merchandise and then sells it to a fence for a profit. A "fence" is someone who knowingly buys illegally obtained goods from a "booster" and then sells the goods for a profit. For more information on organized retail crime, see CRS Report R41118, *Organized Retail Crime*, by Kristin M. Finklea.

117 Charles I. Miller, *Organized Retail Theft: Raising Awareness, Offering Solutions*, National Retail Federation Foundation, 2005, p. 4. See also Food Marketing Institute, *Media Reports—Middle East Connection: Organized Retail Crime*, http://www.fmi.org/docs /loss/ORCMiddleEast.pdf. See also testimony by David Johnson, Section Chief, Criminal Investigative Division, Federal Bureau of Investigation, before the U.S. Congress, House Committee on the Judiciary, Subcommittee on Crime, Terrorism, and Homeland Security, *Combating Organized Retail Crime: The Role of Federal Law Enforcement*, 111th Cong., 1st sess., November 5, 2009.

118 Fiscal impacts are just one of three main types of economic effects, along with the effect of migration on native-born wages and its effect on economic growth.

119 See CRS Report R42053, *Fiscal Impacts of the Foreign-Born Population*, by William A. Kandel.

120 For a discussion of motive or purpose, see Treverton, *Intelligence*, pp. 22-23.

121 In its *SNRA*, DHS made an explicit decision *not* to make this valuation. See DHS, *SNRA*, p. 2.

122 The U.S. Visitor and Immigrant Status Indicator Technology (US-VISIT) program manages DHS's biometric identification services. At ports of entry, CBP officers use US-VISIT technology to capture biometric data (digital fingerprints) from certain incoming travelers, to match the data against information provided during the visa application process, and to check travelers against certain biometric watchlists. For a fuller discussion see CRS Report

R42644, *Department of Homeland Security: FY2013 Appropriations*, coordinated by William L. Painter; and archived CRS Report RL32234, *U.S. Visitor and Immigrant Status Indicator Technology (US-VISIT) Program*, by Lisa M. Seghetti and Stephen R. Vina.

[123] See P.L. 109-367, §(2)(b).

[124] See for example, testimony by Doris Meissner, Director, U.S. Immigration Policy Program, Migration Policy Institute, before the U.S. Congress, Senate Committee on Homeland Security and Governmental Affairs, *Securing the Border: Building on the Progress Made*, 112th Cong., 1st sess., March 30, 2011.

[125] Secure Communities is an information sharing program between the Departments of Justice and Homeland Security. Under the program, when participating law enforcement agencies submit the fingerprints of people being booked into jails to the Federal Bureau of Investigation (FBI) for criminal background checks, the fingerprints also are automatically checked against DHS databases, and potential matches are forwarded to ICE's Law Enforcement Support Center (LESC). When the LESC determines that the arrestee may be a removable alien, information may be forwarded to local ICE field offices, which may initiate removal proceedings against such aliens. For a fuller discussion, see CRS Report R42057, *Interior Immigration Enforcement: Programs Targeting Criminal Aliens*, by Marc R. Rosenblum and William A. Kandel.

[126] One recent study found that illegal inflows fell about 60 percent between 2004 and 2010, with 40% of the reduction due to a stronger Mexican economy, 30% of the reduction due to increased U.S. border enforcement, and 30% of the reduction due to the weaker U.S. economy; see Scott Borger, Gordon Hanson, and Bryan Roberts "The Decision to Emigrate From Mexico," presentation at the Society of Government Economists annual conference, November 6 2012.

[127] As noted above, uncertainty about the likelihood of different illegal flows and inherent subjectivity about their consequences mean there is no "right" answer to this question.

In: Risk Management …
Editor: Gustav Knudsen
ISBN: 978-1-62618-701-6

Chapter 2

RISK MANAGEMENT FUNDAMENTALS*

U.S. Department of Homeland Security

LETTER FROM THE UNDER SECRETARY NATIONAL PROTECTION AND PROGRAMS DIRECTORATE

In May 2010, the Secretary of Homeland Security established a Policy for Integrated Risk Management (IRM). Central to this policy is the premise that security partners can most effectively manage risk by working together, and that management capabilities must be built, sustained, and integrated with Federal, state, local, tribal, territorial, nongovernmental, and private sector homeland security partners. While successful integration requires implementation across the entire homeland security enterprise, the Department of Homeland Security (DHS) plays an essential role in leading the unified effort to manage risks to the Nation from a diverse and complex set of hazards, including acts of terrorism, natural and manmade disasters, pandemics, cyber attacks, and transnational crime.

An essential first step in the integration of risk management is the establishment of doctrine and guidance. *Risk Management Fundamentals* is the first in a series of publications that will provide a structured approach for the distribution and employment of risk information and analysis efforts across the Department. While this is the capstone publication for homeland security

* This is an edited, reformatted and augmented version of U.S. Department of Homeland Security, dated April 2011.

risk management, implementation of risk management requires the combined efforts of Components to tailor and implement key risk management methods and practices. Homeland security risk management is on a positive trajectory and this publication will further enable DHS to mature and strengthen its capabilities to address homeland security risks. The key objectives of this publication are to promote a common understanding of and approach to risk management for homeland security; establish a common foundation that enables consistent risk management application and training; and support the development of a risk management culture and philosophy across DHS. *Risk Management Fundamentals* establishes doctrine for DHS, although concepts within the doctrine may be a useful guide to our Federal interagency partners, state and local agencies, as well as the larger homeland security community.

Risk Management Fundamentals, produced by the Office of Risk Management and Analysis, in coordination with the Office of Policy, has been vetted and approved by the DHS Risk Steering Committee, a governing body of which I serve as the Chairman. Pursuant to the authority vested in the Under Secretary for the National Protection and Programs Directorate by the Secretary of Homeland Security in Delegation Number 17001 to lead the Department's efforts to establish a common framework to address the overall management and analysis of homeland security risk, this publication is hereby recognized and approved for official use until revised or superseded.

Rand Beers
Under Secretary
National Protection and Programs Directorate
Department of Homeland Security

I. KEY OBJECTIVES

This doctrine, *Risk Management Fundamentals*, serves as an authoritative statement regarding the principles and process of homeland security risk management and what they mean to homeland security planning and execution. It is intended as the capstone doctrine on risk management for the Department of Homeland Security (DHS). Furthermore, *Risk Management Fundamentals* serves as a foundational document supporting DHS risk management efforts in partnership with the homeland security enterprise.[1]

Risk Management Fundamentals is intended to help homeland security leaders, supporting staffs, program managers, analysts, and operational personnel develop a framework to make risk management an integral part of planning, preparing, and executing organizational missions. The development of homeland security risk management doctrine is an essential element in promoting a risk-informed culture enabling training, capability development, and integration across DHS to strengthen and improve the Nation's security. *Risk Management Fundamentals* articulates a desired end-state that DHS aspires to achieve in promoting risk management.

This doctrine is not a substitute for independent thought or innovation in applying these principles and concepts. Simply reading the doctrine will not make one adept in managing risks, nor will attempting to follow the ideas herein as if they were a checklist; rather, doctrine serves to shape how one thinks about the issues that you are considering and should be applied based on the operating environment. Homeland security practitioners should compare the doctrine herein against their own experience and think about why, when, and how it applies to their situation and area of responsibility.

Purpose

- Promote a common understanding of, and approach to, risk management;
- Establish organizational practices that should be followed by DHS Components;
- Provide a foundation for conducting risk assessments and evaluating risk management options;
- Set the doctrinal underpinning for institutionalizing a risk management culture through consistent application and training on risk management principles and practices; and
- Educate and inform homeland security stakeholders in risk management applications, including the assessment of capability, program, and operational performance, and the use of such assessments for resource and policy decisions.

A Note on the Scope and Application of this Document

Risk Management Fundamentals captures the theoretical underpinnings of homeland security risk management and articulates principles and practices that should be strived for across homeland security decision making.

In doing so, this document should not be read as criteria to be evaluated against, but instead as a statement of aspirations for improved homeland security decision making, applied in a variety of operating environments, many of which face constraints.

Audience

The principal audiences for *Risk Management Fundamentals* are DHS employees, including:

- Executives who establish strategic and operational priorities, select courses of action, and allocate resources;
- Program Managers and Planners who turn executive decisions into actionable, implementable plans and oversee the day-to-day execution of these plans;
- Operational Personnel who implement plans and programs using specific, tactical and operational risk management tools; and
- Risk and Decision Analysts who collect, assess, and present risk information to help executives make decisions, aid program managers and planners in explaining decisions and approaches to stakeholders, and assist operational personnel in connecting their work to the desired outcome.

Risk Management Fundamentals may be helpful to Federal interagency partners, state and local agencies, as well as the larger homeland security community.

II. Introduction

> ". . . a safe and secure homeland must mean more than preventing terrorist attacks from being carried out. It must also ensure that the liberties of all Americans are assured, privacy is protected, and the means by which we interchange with the world — through travel, lawful immigration, trade, commerce, and exchange — are secured. Ultimately, homeland security is about effectively managing risks to the Nation's security."
>
> ~ *Quadrennial Homeland Security Review* Report, 2010

Homeland Security Risks

The United States homeland security environment is complex and filled with competing requirements, interests, and incentives that must be balanced and managed effectively to ensure the achievement of key national objectives. The safety, security, and resilience of the Nation are threatened by an array of hazards, including acts of terrorism, malicious activity in cyberspace, pandemics, manmade accidents, transnational crime, and natural disasters. At the same time, homeland security organizations must manage risks[2] associated with workforce management, acquisitions operations, and project costs. Collectively, these external and internal risks have the potential to cause loss of life, injuries, negative psychosocial impact, environmental degradation, loss of economic activity, reduction of ability to perform mission essential functions, and loss of confidence in government capabilities. It is the role of DHS and its partners to understand and manage these myriad homeland security risks. We live in a dynamic and uncertain world where the past does not serve as a complete guide to the future. In addition, the systems that provide the functions essential for a thriving society are increasingly intricate and interconnected. This means that potential disruptions to a system are not fully understood and can have large and unanticipated cascading effects throughout American security. Compounding this complexity is the fact that future trends — such as technological advancements, global climate change, asymmetric threats, and the evolving nature of Nation-states — have the potential to significantly alter the homeland security risk landscape in unexpected ways. Yet such emerging trends hold promise as well as peril and should be understood and managed.

Sound Decision Making

Establishing the capability and capacity to identify, understand, and address such complex challenges and opportunities is the crux of risk management. Risk management is an approach for making and implementing improved homeland security decisions.

> "Risk management is the process for identifying, analyzing, and communicating risk and accepting, avoiding, transferring, or controlling it to an acceptable level considering associated costs and benefits of any actions taken." - *DHS Risk Lexicon, 2010 Edition*

To improve decision making, leaders in DHS and their partners in the homeland security enterprise must practice foresight and work to understand known and uncertain risks, as best they can, in order to make sound management decisions. These leaders need to consider the risks facing the homeland to make appropriate resource tradeoffs and align management approaches. Addressing these risks and promoting security is a shared responsibility that depends on unity of effort among Federal, state, local, tribal and territorial governments, the private sector, non-governmental organizations, and the citizenry as a whole.

The Value of Risk Management

The Secretary of Homeland Security has established the requirement for DHS to build and promote an integrated approach to homeland security risk management, working with partners across the homeland security enterprise. The Department's role in establishing integrated risk management is to build security, safety, and resilience across domains by connecting efforts to prevent terrorism and enhance security, secure and manage our borders, enforce and administer our immigration laws, safeguard and secure cyberspace, ensure resilience to disasters, and provide essential support in assuring national and economic security.

Improved homeland security depends on connecting information about risks, activities, and capabilities and using this information to guide prevention, protection, response, and recovery efforts. The establishment of sound risk management practices across DHS and the homeland security enterprise will help protect and enhance national interests, conserve resources, and assist in avoiding or mitigating the effects of emerging or unknown risks. At the organizational level, the application of risk management will complement and augment strategic and operational planning efforts, policy development, budget formulation, performance evaluation and assessments, and reporting processes.

Risk management will not preclude adverse events from occurring; however, it enables national homeland security efforts to focus on those things that are likely to bring the greatest harm, and employ approaches that are likely to mitigate or prevent those incidents. Furthermore, the American people, resources, economy, and way of life are bolstered and made more for hazards, both internal and external, through comprehensive and deliberate risk management.

Resilience and Risk Management

One of the foundational concepts of homeland security is the need to build resilient systems, communities, and institutions that are robust, adaptable and have the capacity for rapid recovery. Resilience and risk management are mutually reinforcing concepts.

Risk management contributes to the achievement of resilience by identifying opportunities to build resilience into planning and resourcing to achieve risk reduction in advance of a hazard, as well as enabling the mitigation of consequences of any disasters that do occur.

Risk management is not an end in and of itself, but rather part of sound organizational practices that include planning, preparedness, program evaluation, process improvement, and budget priority development. The value of a risk management approach or strategy to course of action, but rather in the ability to distinguish between various choices within the larger context. Establishing the infrastructure and organizational culture to support the execution of homeland security risk management is a critical requirement for achieving the Nation's security goals. Risk management is essential for homeland security leaders in prioritizing competing requirements and enabling comprehensive approaches to measure performance and detail progress.

Risk Management Applications

The practice of risk management allows for a systematic and comprehensive approach to homeland security decision making. Risk management promotes the development and use of risk analysis[3] to inform homeland security decision making, to better inform selection among alternative strategies and actions, and to evaluate the effectiveness of the activities we undertake. Risk management applications include:

Strategic Planning

Homeland security strategies should be designed to address the risks that a particular organization faces, taking a long-term view to building capabilities that can mitigate risk through prevention, protection, response, and recovery activities. Homeland security strategies should shape how organizations approach building and sustaining capabilities.

Capabilities-based Planning

Risk management allows planners to prioritize which capabilities might have the greatest return on investment in preparedness activities. Risk management can also help identify which capabilities are most relevant to an organization and identify potential capability gaps.

Resource Decisions

Risk management should be a key component of an evidence-driven approach to requesting and allocating resources, including grant funding. By understanding risk, organizations can identify realistic capability requirements, fund projects that bring the greatest return on investment, describe desired outcomes and how they will mitigate risk, and explain the rationale behind those decisions in clear, objective, and transparent terms.

Operational Planning

Through risk management, organizations can better understand which scenarios are more likely to impact them, what the consequences would be, what risks merit special attention, what actions must be planned for, and what resources are likely to be needed, as well as what risks have the ability to negatively impact operations.

Exercise Planning

Risk management can be used to identify realistic scenarios for exercises, zeroing in on special threats and hazards, as well as priority capabilities and applicable assets.

Real-world Events

Risk management can help decision makers weigh potential courses of action within a contextual understanding of the risk of different threats and hazards to critical assets, geographic areas, and population centers during a crisis.

Research and Development

Risk analysis can be used to inform decisions on filling homeland security gaps and identifying opportunities that may be best met with enhanced technologies and/or innovative solutions, thereby establishing priorities for long-term research and development investments.

III. Homeland Security Risk Management Tenets and Principles

Risk management enables homeland security leaders to distinguish between and among alternative actions, assess capabilities, and prioritize activities and associated resources by understanding risk and its impact on their decisions.

Standard risk management principles are not designed to promote uniformity or conformity; rather, they offer broad guidance that should be uniquely tailored for the specific needs of each organization. While a "one-size-fits-all" approach for homeland security risk management is neither feasible nor desirable, all DHS risk management programs should be based on two ***key tenets***:

- Risk management should enhance an organization's overall decision making process and maximize its ability to achieve its objectives.
- Risk management is used to shape and control risk, but cannot eliminate all risk.

The ***key principles*** for effective risk management include:

- Unity of Effort
- Transparency
- Adaptability
- Practicality
- Customization

A description of each principle follows:

Unity of Effort: *The principal of unity of effort reiterates that homeland security risk management is an enterprise-wide process and should promote integration and synchronization with entities that share responsibility for managing risks.*

Risk management efforts should be coordinated and integrated among all partners, with shared or overlapping risk management responsibilities, to include Federal, state, local, tribal, and territorial governments, as well as the private sector, non-governmental organizations, and international partners. Most homeland security measures involve representatives of different organizations, and it is important that there is unity of effort amongst those charged with managing risks to ensure consistent approaches are taken and that there is a shared perspective of security challenges.

Transparency: *The principle of transparency establishes that effective homeland security risk management depends on open and direct communications.*

Transparency is vitally important in homeland security risk management due to the extent to which the decisions involved affect a broad range of stakeholders. Transparency is important for the analysis that contributes to the decision making. It includes the assumptions that supported that analysis, the uncertainty involved with it, and the communications that follow the decision. Risk management should not be a "black box" exercise where analysis is hidden. Those impacted by a risk management approach should be able to validate the integrity of the approach.

This principle does not countermand the times when there is need for security of sensitive or classified information; however, it does suggest that the processes and methodologies used for homeland security risk management may be shared even if the information is not. In turn, transparency will foster honest and realistic dialogue about opportunities and limitations.

Adaptability*: The principle of adaptability includes designing risk management actions, strategies, and processes to remain dynamic and responsive to change.*

The homeland security landscape is constantly evolving as priorities, threats, and circumstances change, requiring DHS to adapt to meet the Nation's expectations and requirements. DHS and its homeland security partners must be flexible in their approach to managing risk. This means that homeland security solutions must be dynamic. A changing world, filled with adaptive adversaries, increased interdependencies, and new technologies, necessitates security measures that are equally adaptable.

Practicality: *The principle of practicality pertains to the acknowledgement that homeland security risk management cannot eliminate all uncertainty nor is it reasonable to expect to identify all risks and their likelihood and consequences.*

The limitations of managing homeland security risk arises from the dynamic nature of homeland security threats, vulnerabilities, and consequences, as well as the uncertainty that is generally associated with assessing risks. This is especially true when facing a threat from an adaptive adversary, such as a terrorist or criminal organization.

Homeland security decisions often are made amidst uncertainty, but that uncertainty does not preclude the need for sound analysis or well thought-out and structured decision making. Risk management is an effective and important management practice that should lead to better-supported decisions and more effective programs and operations.

Customization: *The principle of customization emphasizes that risk management programs should be tailored to match the needs and culture of the organization, while being balanced with the specific decision environment they support.*

DHS organizations and personnel should tailor the methods for the dissemination of risk information and decision making and communications processes to fit the needs of their mission. The customization principle includes ensuring that the organization's risk management approach is appropriately governed and uses the best available information. This assures that the risk management effort is systematic, timely, and structured based on the values of the organization. However, the principle of customization does not supersede the need to adhere to organizational standards, requirements, and operating procedures for risk management when there is a requirement for working together to analyze risks and promote joint decision making.

IV. A Comprehensive Approach to Risk Management

DHS decision makers should employ a comprehensive approach to understanding and managing risks so that they can enhance the quality of decisions throughout their organization[4] — thus supporting the DHS Policy for Integrated Risk Management.[5] Doing so serves to improve decision making by allowing organizations to attempt to balance internal and external sources of risk to achieve their strategy. This section identifies the types of risks facing DHS organizations, and sets forth some necessary practices for managing these risks in an understandable way.

Internal Sources of Risk

Risks impacting organizational effectiveness arise from both internal and external sources. Examples of internal sources are issues such as financial stewardship, personnel reliability, and systems reliability. Organizations across government and the private sector are all subject to these types of internal risks.

These internal risks have the potential to derail effective operations and adversely affect mission accomplishment.

A comprehensive approach to risk management serves to identify weaknesses and assists in creating internal systems and processes that minimize the potential for mission failure.

External Sources of Risk

Many organizations have additional risks to manage that are caused by external factors.

Examples include global, political, and societal trends, as well as hazards from natural disasters, terrorism, malicious activity in cyberspace, pandemics, transnational crime, and manmade accidents.

It is these hazards and threats that caused the Nation to make a significant commitment in homeland security, and it is important that the risks from external threats remain at the forefront of consideration for homeland security organizations.

> "Threat is a natural or man-made occurrence, individual, entity, or action that has or indicates the potential to harm life, information, operations, the environment, and/or property."
>
> - *DHS Risk Lexicon, 2010 Edition*

Organizations should implement comprehensive risk management approaches to ensure all internal and external risks are considered in a holistic way.

Organizations must manage risks as a system, while considering the underlying factors that directly impact organizational effectiveness and mission success.

In order to consider the whole of homeland security risks, the categories in the following table help to define the landscape for an organization as it establishes a comprehensive approach to risk management.

Identifying and understanding risks and their interactions ensures DHS leaders have a more complete perspective to manage risks and promote organizational effectiveness.

Organizational Risk Categories

	Strategic Risks	Operational Risks	Institutional Risks
Definition	Risk that affects an organization's vital interests or execution of a chosen strategy, whether imposed by external threats or arising from flawed or poorly implemented strategy.	Risk that has the potential to impede the successful execution of operations with existing resources, capabilities, and strategies.	Risk associated with an organization's ability to develop and maintain effective management practices, control systems, and flexibility and adaptability to meet organizational requirements.
Description	These risks threaten an organization's ability to achieve its strategy, as well as position itself to recognize, anticipate, and respond to future trends, conditions, and challenges. Strategic risks include those factors that may impact the organization's overall objectives and long-term goals.	Operational risks include those that impact personnel, time, materials, equipment, tactics, techniques, information, technology, and procedures that enable an organization to achieve its mission objectives.	These risks are less obvious and typically come from within an organization. Institutional risks include factors that can threaten an organization's ability to organize, recruit, train, support, and integrate the organization to meet all specified operational and administrative requirements.

Key Business Practices

Effective management of risk is fostered and executed through a few key requirements. First and foremost, an organization must employ risk management with commitment and active participation by its leadership. If decision makers within an organization fully endorse and prioritize risk management practices, then employees at all levels will strive to understand and adopt risk management principles. Furthermore, risk management is only effective if it is used to inform decision making. This means that for risk management efforts to be successful, leaders must support risk management practices and incorporate risk information into their decision making.

Second, managing risk requires a consistent approach across the organization. Although processes do not need to be identical, they should facilitate the ability to compare risks, as required, across the organization and provide reasonable assurance that risk management can be conducted coherently. Managing risk as a system allows for greater situational awareness of how varied risks and mitigation efforts may impact other activities.

Third, an organization must be able to view risk on a comprehensive, enterprise-wide basis.

Most risk information is viewed by the individuals responsible for managing particular risks, who are not necessarily able to see how risks can affect other parts of the organization or to see the cumulative risks the organization faces.

Thus, an organization requires some sort of function that allows for information to cascade up, providing its leadership with an organization-wide view of its risks so as to promote better tradeoff decisions and enhance application of foresight.

V. The Homeland Security Risk Management Process

To bolster common, interoperable, and systematic approaches to risk management, DHS organizations should employ a standardized risk management process.[6]

This approach promotes comparability and a shared understanding of information and analysis in the decision process, and facilitates better structured and informed decision making.

The homeland security risk management process should be implemented while keeping in mind the previously articulated risk management principles.

The process is comprised of the following:

- Defining and framing the context of decisions and related goals and objectives;
- *Identifying the risks* associated with the goals and objectives;
- *Analyzing and assessing* the identified risks;
- *Developing alternative actions* for managing the risks and creating opportunities, and analyzing the costs and benefits of those alternatives;
- *Making a decision* among alternatives and *implementing that decision*; and
- *Monitoring* the implemented decision and comparing observed and expected effects to help influence subsequent risk management alternatives and decisions.

DHS Risk Management Process.

Risk Communications

The foundation for each element of the risk management process is effective communications with stakeholders, partners, and customers. Consistent, two-way communication throughout the process helps ensure that the decision maker, analysts, and ultimately those charged to implement any decision share a common understanding of what the risk is and what factors may contribute to managing it. The concepts of uncertainty, perception, and tolerance for loss, which are intertwined with the concept of risk, should be accounted for as part of this communication. Effective communication is also an essential element in executing adopted courses of action and in explaining risks and risk management decisions to external parties such as the public. Such external communications may occur throughout the risk management process and should be considered integral to effective risk management.

Risk Management Processes

The homeland security risk management process supports every mission of DHS and partner organizations and is generally compatible with other documented risk management processes. These include other risk management frameworks and standards promulgated by transnational organizations and other governments.[7] Although it is influenced by all of those approaches, this process is specifically designed for the totality of the homeland security mission and is intended to be utilized to provide DHS with a standard process for risk management.

Elements of the Homeland Security Risk Management Process

Risk management supports a spectrum of homeland security decisions, including strategic planning, standards and doctrine development, policy formulation, budget and resource allocation, program implementation, program evaluation and assessment, research and development investments, short-term operational activities, and problem-solving. The sections that follow describe all the steps in the application of the risk management process to support such decision making. However, the realities of an organization's environment dictate that, at times, implementing the six-step risk management process may not be a linear progression. Program managers, operational personnel, analysts, and decision makers may be required to improvise and truncate steps in the process based on time and resource constraints. For example, to support operations such as law enforcement efforts and incident management activities, this risk management process is often executed in a less structured or expedited manner. In a tactical setting, such as law enforcement activities, circumstances may require that the decision cycle be completed in a matter of seconds. This is the reality of the homeland security operating environment and the necessity that comes with reacting swiftly during times of stress. Note that even when the risk management process is expedited or cannot be sequentially executed, it is still appropriate to continue through the cycle after a decision has been made to allow adjustments in execution and to better evaluate performance. The homeland security risk management process consists of the following sequence of planning and analysis efforts:

1. Define the Context

To execute risk management, it is critical to define the context for the decision that the risk management effort will support. For complex problem-solving, an organization will typically assemble a risk analysis and management team (which are frequently referred to as a planning team, a task force, or a working group, among other descriptions) to help decision makers go through the risk management process. When establishing the context, analysts must understand and document the associated requirements and constraints that will influence the decision making process, as well as key assumptions. While the analysis and management team members do not have to be risk experts, they must gain an understanding of the environment in which the risks are to be managed, taking into account political and policy concerns, mission needs, stakeholder interests, and risk tolerance. Defining the context will inform and shape successive stages of the risk management cycle.

The considerations for defining the context can be as complex and varied as the decisions they are intended to support. The following is intended to offer some structure in scoping the variables to be considered when executing the risk management process, although often times it is not feasible to study all of these factors:

Goals and Objectives

Ensure that the goals and objectives of the risk management effort align with the desired requirements, outcome, or end-state of the decision making process. Clearly defined goals and objectives are essential to identifying, assessing, and managing those areas that may threaten success.

Mission Space and Values

When defining the decision context, consider the mission space and values of the organization and its decision makers.

Policies and Standards

Ensure that risk management efforts complement and take into account any risk management policies, standards, or requirements the organization has in place.

Scope and Criticality of the Decision

Understand the decisions that have to be made, and the range of options available to leaders. The breadth and depth of the decisions' impact must also be considered. The risk analysis and management effort should be commensurate to that criticality.

Decision Makers and Stakeholders

Organizational leaders and their staff must be engaged at the outset of a risk management process so that the approach and presentation of results can be tailored to their preferences. It is also helpful to understand the authorities and responsibilities of leaders, as well as their comfort level with risk management concepts and language.

Similarly, stakeholders — those individuals or groups affected by the decisions — should be appropriately engaged and represented throughout the risk management process to ensure concerns are being addressed. This can be accomplished through direct interaction, such as conferences and public meetings.

Decision Timeframe

The timeframe in which a decision must be made and executed will dictate a number of the attributes of the risk management effort, including how much time is available for conducting formal analysis and decision review. Related to this issue is the frequency of the decision, which can also affect the risk management effort's analytic depth. The time horizon that the decision will impact must also be considered, such as whether the decision will have an influence only in the short-term or over a long period of time.

Risk Management Capabilities and Resources

At the beginning of the risk management process, it is useful to identify the staff, money, skill sets knowledge levels, and other resources available for risk analysis and management efforts. The implemented approach needs to be feasible and aligned with the organization's capabilities, capacity, and processes. Additionally, the resources applied to support the effort should be commensurate with the complexity of the issues involved and the magnitude of the decision. For example, it would be irresponsible to spend significant resources to support a decision with a minimal projected impact.

Risk Tolerance

Determining and understanding the decision makers' general risk tolerance level is helpful before embarking on the risk management process. Risk management efforts often involve tradeoffs between positive and negative outcomes. Having perspective on an organization or a decision maker's risk tolerance will help shape the assessments and the development of risk management alternatives that will be presented to leadership.

Availability and Quality of Information

When evaluating decision requirements, consider the availability and quality of information that can support the risk management effort, as available information will impact the design of the risk analysis approach. In engaging with decision makers at the outset of the risk management cycle, it is important to convey anticipated data limitations, including expected levels of uncertainty, so decision makers can adjust their expectations accordingly.

Designing an Approach

The above considerations shape and help define the design of the required processes to identify risks and conduct risk assessment and analysis and allow for the selection, implementation, and evaluation of risk management alternatives. By considering each of these elements systematically, decision makers and the analysts who support them are able to design an approach that is appropriate given the context.

Additionally, as the risk management process is iterative, the context may be redefined based on external events, shifting priorities, and new information. Considering such change is critical for ensuring that both the principles of flexibility and practicality are adhered to as part of risk management.

2. Identify Potential Risk

For homeland security, there is a need to consider a wide variety of risks to support decision making. As previously noted, these considerations include strategic, operational, and institutional risks. The risks that are included in any particular assessment (sometimes called the assessment's scope) are largely determined by the decision the assessment is designed to inform. The decision context established in the previous step of the process should be used to determine what individual risks should be identified and assessed.

Identifying a preliminary list of risks can generally be done from a basic knowledge of the subject matter of the decision. To do so, it is sometimes helpful to think about the risks in terms of "risk to" and "risk from." This can be a very simple exercise of defining elements affected (goals, objectives, and systems) to determine the "risk to" and capturing the things (hazards, resources, and institutional failures) that impact them to determine the "risk from." This approach will yield a fairly broad list of potentially adverse outcomes that will assist in the identification of mitigation efforts and resources.

Unusual, Unlikely, and Emerging Risks

Prior to conducting a risk assessment, it is valuable to make a concerted effort to identify risks beyond those usually considered. For example, risks that are newly developing, even if they are poorly understood, are useful to identify. Risks that are highly unlikely but have high consequences should also be identified and incorporated into the assessment, if possible. This can even include identifying the risk of the unknown as a possible risk. Brainstorming is a common technique to identify these unusual, emerging, and rare risks. So, too, is involving a wide range of perspectives and strategic thinkers to avoid the trap of conventional wisdom and groupthink. Even when a risk is difficult to assess, it may still be important to try to understand and should be noted. It should also be acknowledged that no identification of risks is likely to capture every potential unwanted outcome — there will always be things that happen that are unanticipated.

Scenarios

It is generally appropriate and helpful for homeland security risk assessments to use scenarios to divide the identified risks into separate pieces that can be assessed and analyzed individually.

> A scenario is a "hypothetical situation comprised of a hazard, an entity impacted by that hazard, and associated conditions including consequences when appropriate." - *DHS Risk Lexicon, 2010 Edition*

When developing scenarios to identify potential risks for a risk assessment, the set of scenarios should attempt to cover the full scope of the assessment to ensure that the decision maker is provided with complete information when making a decision. Also, the scenarios should not overlap, as including multiple scenarios that contain the same event may lead to double counting the risk. Organizing the identified risks into a framework, such as with scenarios, is helpful preparation for creating a viable methodology in the next step in the risk management cycle. In addition, examining the risks in a structured way can also be used to identify gaps where potential risks have been left out.

3. Assess and Analyze Risk

The purpose of this step is to assess the identified risks and analyze the outputs of the assessment. This step consists of several tasks:

- Determining a methodology;
- Gathering data;
- Executing the methodology;
- Validating and verifying the data; and
- Analyzing the outputs.

In practice, these tasks, like the steps of the larger risk management cycle, rarely occur linearly. Instead, risk practitioners often move back and forth between the tasks, such as refining a methodology after some data has been gathered.

Methodology

When choosing a risk assessment methodology, care should be given to remaining within the organization's capabilities.[8]

> **"Methodology"** is used in this document to mean any logical process by which the inputs into an assessment are processed to produce the outputs that inform the decision.

The most important factor to consider in selecting a methodology is the decision the assessment must inform. The methodology should only be as complex as necessary to properly inform the decision.

In homeland security risk analysis, there are a large number of pre-existing methodologies that may be appropriately applied to similar decisions. However, some homeland security risk management decisions will require novel methodologies, as this is a new and quickly developing field. Hence, when trying to determine the methodology, assessments that have already been completed may be a good starting point but should not be considered as the only options. Though properly informing the decision is the prime factor when selecting a methodology, other concerns will also influence the choice. Data availability, as well as time, financial, and personnel constraints also play a role.

Likelihood and Consequences

Homeland security risks can be assessed in terms of their likelihood and consequences.

> **Likelihood** is the chance of something happening, whether defined, measured or estimated in terms of general descriptors, frequencies, or probabilities.
>
> **Consequence**, or impact, is the effect of an incident, event, or occurrence, whether direct or indirect. In homeland security risk analysis, consequences include (but are not limited to) loss of life, injuries, economic impacts, psychological consequences, environmental degradation, and inability to execute essential missions.
>
> - *DHS Risk Lexicon, 2010 Edition*

There is no single methodology that is appropriate for measuring the likelihood and consequences of every homeland security risk, and each methodology requires independent judgment regarding its design. In some cases, it may not even be necessary to explicitly determine likelihood and consequence.

Many homeland security risk assessments consider homeland security risks as a function[9] of *Threats, Vulnerabilities, and Consequences (TVC).* Explicitly considering each of the TVC factors is appropriate for many homeland security risks, such as those related to infrastructure protection.[10]

However, considering TVC explicitly is sometimes not the best approach for other homeland security risk assessments — especially those that include institutional risks that can impact an organization's ability to meet operational and administrative requirements. In fact, one of the most common mistakes in homeland security risk analysis is misapplying the TVC framework. It is important that the TVC

framework be applied only when appropriate to the subject matter of the analysis and the character of the assessed risks. In addition, analysts should be very careful when calculating risk by multiplying threats, vulnerabilities, and consequences, especially for terrorism, because interdependencies between the three variables, and/or poorly executed mathematical operations, can lead to inaccurate results.[11]

Types of Methodologies

As a general rule, simple, but defensible, methodologies are preferred over more complicated methods. Simple methodologies are less prone to errors and are easier for stakeholders to understand. They are also more likely to fulfill the principles of transparency and practicality.

Homeland security risk methodologies are often sorted into qualitative[12] and quantitative[13] categories, but when well-designed, both types of assessments have the potential to deliver useful analytic results.[14]

Similarly, both qualitative and quantitative methodologies can be needlessly complex or poorly designed.

As stated previously, the methodology that best meets the decision maker's needs is generally the best choice, whether quantitative or qualitative.

Gathering Data

Once a methodology for informing the decision has been determined, data must be gathered to populate the assessment. There are a number of potential sources for risk information. Some of the most commonly used sources for homeland security risk assessments include historical records, models, simulations, and elicitations of subject matter experts.

Elicitations involve using structured questions to gather information from individuals with in-depth knowledge of specific areas or fields. They are typically used when the historical record is either nonexistent or is not appropriate for collecting data on a specific scenario.

When collecting data, attention should be paid to all aspects of the decision that are important, regardless of whether these aspects can be readily quantified. For example, when considering the consequences of strategic homeland security risks, the assessed consequences may include difficult-to-quantify psychological impacts in addition to consequences such as lives lost and economic damage. Structured techniques, such as value focused thinking, can help the analyst determine which aspects of consequences should be included in the methodology.

Many pieces of data are not known precisely. For example, the cost estimate for damage resulting from a major earthquake in California can be estimated by a subject matter expert to fall within a range, with some values being more likely than others. The assumptions and uncertainty in the inputs should be considered in each step of the assessment's methodology to determine how they affect the outputs. Uncertainty in the outputs should then be communicated to the decision maker, as well as the assumptions that underpin the analysis. It is also useful to consider the impact of the uncertainty and how sensitive the assessment of risk is to particular pieces of uncertain data.

Validation and Presentation

Throughout the process of executing the assessment, the gathered data and evidence should be carefully studied and compared to previous work — as should the results — as doing so is part of validation and verification.

Decision makers will rarely be well-served by only a simple presentation of the outputs of a risk assessment, so the data and evidence should be analyzed to identify relevant and interesting features to the decision maker. In a broad assessment, the decision maker will often have specific areas they are particularly interested in, and will ask the analysts to focus in on those areas. Follow-up analyses will then need to be completed. In this way, analysts will regularly iterate a cycle of analyzing risks and presenting the analysis to decision makers.

Integrating Alternatives

Often, the evaluation of alternative risk management actions is part of a risk assessment methodology. Though the development of alternatives is the next step in the risk management cycle, many homeland security leaders prefer the alternatives to be integrated into the risk assessment, necessitating additional data collection and analysis. The earlier in the process the potential alternatives are known, the more efficiently their data collection can be integrated into the data collection for the rest of the assessment.

4. Develop Alternatives

In order to improve the country's ability to prevent, protect against, respond to, recover from, and mitigate a variety of manmade and natural hazards, homeland security leaders must focus their attention on identifying and executing actions to manage homeland security risks. Ultimately, the objective of homeland security risk analysis is to provide decision makers with a structured way to identify and choose risk management actions.

Identifying and Assessing Options

Within the risk management process, the step of developing alternatives involves systematically identifying and assessing available risk management options. Portions of this step may be performed by different practitioners, but the alternatives development phase brings together proposed risk management actions with the results of a risk assessment, to include course-of-action comparisons. This provides leaders with a clear picture of the risk management benefits of each proposed action or group of actions. The picture of potential benefits, when combined with an analysis of an action's costs — both monetary and non-monetary — can serve as a valuable resource for aiding decision makers in making effective and efficient homeland security choices.

Ultimately, the development of alternative risk management actions should:

- Be understandable to participants of the process, including the decision makers and stakeholders;
- Match and comply with the organization's relevant doctrine, standards, and plans;
- Provide documentation with assumptions explicitly detailed;
- Allow for future refinements; and

- Include planning for assessment of progress toward achieving desired outcomes.

Risk Management Strategies

Risk management actions include strategies, treatments, or countermeasures for managing risks. Risks can be managed by one of four distinct methods: *risk acceptance, risk avoidance, risk control,* and *risk transfer.*[15]

Risk Management Strategies

	Definition
Risk Acceptance	An explicit or implicit decision not to take an action that would affect a particular risk.[16]
Risk Avoidance	A strategy or measure which effectively removes the exposure of an organization to a risk.
Risk Control (or reduction)	Deliberate actions taken to reduce a risk's potential for harm or maintain the risk at an acceptable level.
Risk Transfer (or deflection)	Shifting some or all of the risk to another entity, asset, system, network, or geographic area.

Methods for Developing and Evaluating Alternatives

Developing and evaluating alternative courses of action involves both technical study and applied ingenuity. While approaches for developing and evaluating alternatives are as diverse as the problem sets, considerations may include:

- Reviewing lessons learned from relevant past incidents;
- Consulting subject matter experts, best practices and government guidelines;
- Brainstorming;
- Organizing risk management actions;
- Evaluating options for risk reduction and residual risk;
- Developing cost estimates for risk management actions;
- Comparing the benefit of each risk management action with its associated cost; and
- Eliminating potential options.

Evaluating risk management options should involve information generated in the context-setting and risk assessment steps of the risk management cycle.

This information should be generated through analysis of the costs and other negative impacts, as well as the projected benefits of identified courses of action. It is important to note that risk management actions can be evaluated based on their potential to manage risk in the aggregate across a range of scenarios, as well as their ability to manage risks associated with a single scenario; maintaining both perspectives is crucial in identifying the most effective actions.

Needs and Constraints

Alternatives development requires consideration of the needs and constraints of an organization during the decision making process. For example, the team developing alternatives must consider the time needed to implement each risk management option; the objectives of the option, methods to achieve the objectives, and the resources required to implement the option; performance objectives, measures, and targets; and the decision making environment that would influence strategy implementation and sustainability. In a sense, the developing alternatives step is about understanding and clearly communicating the costs and benefits, expected outcomes, and likelihood of success of each strategy option.

Iterative Process

Alternatives development should be treated as a process that is iterative and evolutionary.

Since risks often shift, it is important to revisit the alternatives development process, incorporate new information, and re-evaluate the options based on changed circumstances. Changes in threats or the emergence of a new risk can make a previously discarded risk management option possible, or even preferable to other options.

5. Decide Upon and Implement Risk Management Strategies

Risk management entails making decisions about best options among a number of alternatives in an uncertain environment. The key moment in the execution of any risk management process is when a decision maker[17] chooses among alternatives for managing risks, and makes the decision to implement the selected course of action.

This can include making an affirmative decision to implement a new alternative, as well as the decision to maintain the status quo.

Presenting Information

For the "Decide and Implement" phase, decision makers need to consider the feasibility of implementing options, and how various alternatives affect and reduce risk. This includes the consideration of adequate resources, capabilities, time to implement, policy imperatives, legal issues, the potential impact on stakeholders, and the potential for creating new risks for the organization.

When providing decision makers with alternatives, analysts should present options, and their strengths and weaknesses, clearly and understandably in order to ensure that decisions are informed by a common understanding of the organization's risks.

Information should be tailored to the needs of leadership, and the risk analysis and management team should consider who the audience is when preparing to communicate assessments and strategies.

Document and Implement

Once a decision has been made, the decision maker must ensure that the decision is documented and communicated, and that an appropriate management structure is in place to implement the decision. Leadership should require comprehensive project management approaches that will document the planning, organizing, and managing of resources necessary for the successful implementation of the risk management strategy.

This should include identifying metrics for the implementation process, which will allow the organization to track progress and improve future efforts. Additionally, leadership should develop an approach for the management of residual risk to the organization left after the decision.

6. Evaluation and Monitoring

This phase includes the evaluation and monitoring of performance to determine whether the stated goals and objectives. In addition to assessing performance, organizations should guard against unintended adverse impacts, such as creating additional risk or failing to recognize changes in risk characteristics.

The evaluation phase is designed to bring a systematic, disciplined approach to assessing and improving the effectiveness of risk management program implementation. It is not just the improved; it is the actual risk reduction measures themselves.

Evaluation should be conducted in a way that is commensurate with both the level of risk and the scope of the mission.

Logic Models

One way to develop measures that evaluate the implementation of a risk management decision is to build a performance logic model that defines causal relationships between activities and risk management goals. These logic models typically include:

- Risk Management Goals: A description of the overall end-state expected to be achieved in terms of managing identified risks.
- Inputs: A description of the resources that are used to carry out risk management efforts.
- Efforts: A description of the types of efforts or activities that, employing the inputs, work toward achieving the risk management goals.
- Output: A description of what is immediately produced by the activities, including metrics that can be used to measure that production.
- Outcome Performance Measures: A description of the combined effect that delivering outputs are expected to have, including measures that evaluate the impact of the combined efforts in achieving the risk management goals.

Performance Measurement

Organization may find it necessary to adjust its risk management options. It is crucial that a process of performance measurement be established to evaluate whether the actions taken ultimately achieved the intended performance objective. This is important not only in evaluating the success of the implemented option, but also in holding the organization accountable for progress. A core element of evaluating and monitoring risk criteria to track and report on performance results with concrete, realistic metrics. In cases where the chosen course of action is to do nothing, the continued appropriateness of accepting the risk may be the best possible metric. In other cases, the best metric is often the reduction of the likelihood or consequences associated with a risk. It is also important to monitor the larger context within which an identified risk and risk management effort exists. Good situational awareness may reveal changes in the context that require corresponding changes in the risk management effort. Both types of monitoring — effectiveness and situational awareness — are essential if risk management efforts are to be effective over time.

Models of Evaluation

Models of evaluation include red teaming (scenario role-playing), exercises, external review, and surveys. Different models of evaluation will require differing levels of involvement from organization leadership and staff. For example, red teaming and exercises should be guided by leadership and analysts. External review, however, is an independent activity that should not be influenced by the risk management activity under evaluation. Leadership must provide the appropriate and requested information to the external review team, and the process should be conducted in an independent and unbiased manner. The benefit of testing effectiveness using these methods is that it provides different perspectives on the capabilities of the risk management program. It also allows one to validate what is going well, and areas that may need improvement. Evaluating and monitoring implemented risk management strategies should be part of considering overall performance management of homeland security activities.

7. Risk Communications

> *Risk communication* "is the exchange of information with the goal of improving risk understanding, affecting risk perception, and/or equipping people or groups to take appropriate actions in response to an identified risk."
>
> - *DHS Risk Lexicon, 2010 Edition*

Communications underpin the entire risk management process. As explained earlier, homeland security risk is a fluid concept affected by varying perceptions and loss tolerances, as well as uncertainty. As a result, it is imperative that risks and risk management decisions are communicated between stakeholders, partners, and customers. Communication requirements will differ, however, according to the audience and timeframe. Typically, risk communication is divided between internal and external audiences and between incident and standard timeframes.

Internal Risk Communications

Some risk communications are internal to an organization, such as that between analysts and decision makers. Maintaining two-way communication throughout the risk management process ensures that the key principles of risk management are met. For example, decision makers provide context (including values and perceptions) to bound analysts' exploration of risks and meet the organization's goals and objectives. Allowing decision makers input from the beginning of the process improves transparency, creates leadership buy-in, and sets the framework for an assessment tailored appropriately to the organization's needs and objectives. In turn, analysts provide information on risks and on possible actions to address the risks. Being transparent about methodology, limitations, and uncertainty provides decision makers with the most accurate, defensible, and practical information on which to base risk management decisions. Every internal stakeholder in the risk management process — decision makers, analysts, operational personnel, and program managers — should be included in the activities of that process through consistent, two-way communication.

External Risk Communications

The public and cross-agency nature of homeland security risk often necessitates that DHS communicate with external stakeholders, partners, and the public. Risk management decisions should be communicated to the public when appropriate in order to minimize fear while building trust. In addition, other forms of government as well as the public and the private sector often have an important role to play in reducing risk and are therefore an integral part of the risk management process. When communicating to external parties, it is essential that varying risk perceptions and knowledge of risks be taken into account. Those outside the Department sometimes have a different perspective regarding risks than those within the Department, just as decision makers, analysts, operational personnel, and program managers have different perspectives from each other. Such differences mean that communications should be carefully tailored to the audience, but also represent an opportunity to strengthen the risk management process.

External parties may help mold potential alternatives, provide context to the decision, and monitor and evaluate decisions that have been made. Thus external communications should also be two-way and should include an organization's public affairs professionals as appropriate.

Incident vs. Standard Timeframe Communications

How risk communications is defined and employed can differ based on a number of factors, including the relevance of time pressure, the purpose of the message, and the entity responsible for communicating the information. DHS communicates risks on a daily basis. Standard types of risk communications involve little time pressure and are intended to empower decision making among partners, stakeholders and the public.

Incident, or crisis, communications take place under different conditions than standard communications. In a crisis, empowering decision making remains a priority; however, time constraints are a critical consideration and the need to explain and persuade becomes increasingly important as a result of psychological changes in how people take in and act on information and protective guidance. Internal communications should remain bi-directional, but top-down decisiveness takes on greater importance. Externally, it is important that communications to stakeholders, partners, and the public provide clear information and, if appropriate, guidance on actions to take in a manner that is designed to minimize the anxiety that may arise in such a situation.

If the lines of communication have already been established under standard conditions, incident communications will occur more naturally and smoothly, ensuring that DHS and its partners can more effectively prevent, protect, respond, and recover. In addition, both the *National Response Framework* (January 2008) and the *National Incident Management System* (December 2008) call for a Communications Plan to be developed as one of the major components of establishing an Incident Command System and maintaining a common operating picture during an incident.[18]

After an incident, standard communications should resume so that all stakeholders build a common understanding of what has happened, why certain decisions were made, and how to move forward. Essentially, an incident does not represent a break in the risk management process, but rather a temporary acceleration after which the process continues as normal.

Risk Communications Considerations

Risk communications will be most effective if guided by the following interrelated aims:

- *Plan for communications.* Communication efforts for decision makers and stakeholders need to be proactive as part of the risk management process; they should not be "tacked on" at the end as an afterthought. Furthermore, risk information needs to be readily available for relevant parties at all stages of the risk management cycle.
- *Maintain trust.* Past communication efforts give context to the organization's next message, shaping how it will be received. Consistency is important, but only as long as it serves to build trust. When consistency is untenable in light of emerging information, then officials need to acknowledge it, including any errors that may be

involved, and explain it. Once trust is lost, it is very difficult to recover.

- *Use language appropriate to the audience.* When communicating risk, it is important to consider the intended audience and tailor the language and channels used to effectively convey the information to promote and elicit the desired actions and outcomes.
- *Be both clear and transparent.* Clarity and transparency are important to effective communications. Clarity means communicating in a direct, simple and understandable way. Transparency in communications means disclosing assumptions, methodology, and uncertainty considered.
- *Respect the audience's concerns.* Risk communications are most effective when the recipient's concerns and/or issues are acknowledged. Maintaining open channels for collaboration or feedback fosters mutual understanding. Communicators should be both receptive and responsive to queries from decision makers and stakeholders.
- *Maintain integrity of information.* Effective risk communications should acknowledge uncertainty, note any limitations of information, make assumptions explicit, and distinguish assertions from judgments supported by analysis and evidence.

Communication connects each step of the risk management process. It is also crucial for linking the risk management principles and process. One cannot overstate the importance of risk communications in risk management.

CONCLUSION

This document serves as doctrine to define the principles, process and operational practices of effective homeland security risk management and is intended for DHS organizations and personnel to adopt and employ. Applying consistent doctrine that promotes the understanding of sound risk management practices is a critical step toward creating a cohesive approach to homeland security.

In order to promote and enhance the safety, security, and resilience of the Nation, DHS leaders and their homeland security partners need to identify, understand, and develop strategies to prevent, mitigate, and control risks. The establishment and sustainment of a risk management culture across DHS and its partners will require continued commitment and attention from leadership and personnel. The development of risk management capabilities requires time, resources, training, and ongoing support by all levels of management. DHS will continue to lead the development and establishment of those capabilities to achieve an integrated approach to homeland security risk management. In doing so, DHS will build on the foundation established by *Risk Management Fundamentals.*

End Notes

[1] As noted in the *2010 Quadrennial Homeland Security Review Report*, the homeland security enterprise "refers to the collective efforts and shared responsibilities of Federal, state, local, tribal, territorial, non-governmental, private volunteer, and privatesector partners — as well as individuals, families, and communities — to maintain critical homeland security capabilities. It connotes a broad-based community with a common interest in the safety and well being of America and American society."

[2] Throughout this document, risk is defined as "the potential for an unwanted outcome resulting from an incident, event, or occurrence, as determined by its likelihood and the associated consequences." *DHS Risk Lexicon, 2010 Edition.*

[3] Risk analysis is the "systematic examination of the components and characteristics of risk." *DHS Risk Lexicon, 2010 Edition.*

[4] Many organizations describe their comprehensive approach to risk management using the term Enterprise Risk Management (ERM), defined as "a comprehensive approach to risk management that engages organizational systems and processes together to improve the quality of decision making for managing risks that may hinder an organization from achieving its objectives." *DHS Risk Lexicon, 2010 Edition.*

5 The concept of Integrated Risk Management was defined in the DHS Secretary's Memorandum, *DHS Policy for Integrated Risk Management*, dated May 27, 2010.

[6] The homeland security risk management process was defined in the DHS Secretary's Memorandum, *DHS Policy for Integrated Risk Management*, dated May 27, 2010. This document incorporates and amplifies that risk management process.

[7] Examples of relevant international standards include the Australian and New Zealand Standard on Risk Management (AS/NZ 4360) and the International Organization for Standardization Principles and Risk Management Standard (ISO 31000).

[8] The National Research Council notes that "Rarely is there a single 'right' risk analysis tool, method or model to provide 'correct' analysis to support decision making. In general, a risk analysis is intended to combine data and modeling techniques with subject matter expertise in a logical fashion to yield outputs that differentiate among decision options and help the decision maker improve his or her decision over what could be accomplished merely with experience and intuition." Committee to Review the Department of Homeland Security's Approach to Risk Analysis, *Review of the Department of Homeland Security's Approach to Risk Analysis*, Washington DC, National Academies Press, 2010, p.94.

[9] "Function" means that a value is assigned to each input of threat, vulnerability, and consequence, and the inputs are considered in combination.

[10] The *National Infrastructure Protection Plan*, published in 2009, calls for infrastructure risks from any scenario to be considered "as a function of consequence, vulnerability, and threat." p. 32.

[11] As the National Academies of Science states: "The definition of Risk = T x V x C makes sense…but not for natural disasters." p. 99.

[12] Qualitative Risk Assessment methodology is defined as "a set of methods, principles, or rules for assessing risk based on non-numerical categories or levels." *DHS Risk Lexicon, 2010 Edition.*

[13] Quantitative Risk Assessment methodology is defined as "a set of methods, principles, or rules for assessing risk based on the use of numbers where the meanings and proportionality of values are maintained inside and outside the context of the assessment." *DHS Risk Lexicon, 2010 Edition.*

[14] The National Research Council notes that "narrative descriptions of non-quantitative information about risk are often as important to decision makers as is the more fully quantitative information." Committee to Review the Department of Homeland Security's Approach to Risk Analysis, *Review of the Department of Homeland Security's Approach to Risk Analysis*, Washington DC, National Academies Press, 2010, p.10.

[15] For more information about these four risk management treatment options see the *DHS Risk Lexicon, 2010 Edition.*

[16] For example, a decision may be made to not invest in a countermeasure because the cost outweighs the risk reduction return on investment. Responsible risk management dictates that for some risks the most appropriate action will be to do nothing and to accept the risk. However, when the "no action" option is chosen, it should not be the result of inattention but of thoughtful analysis and careful consideration of the costs and benefits of alternative courses of action.

[17] Within the homeland security enterprise, decision makers can be anyone from a national official to the head of a local law enforcement agency to a first responder.

[18] For further information on incident communications requirements, see the *National Incident Management System published in December 2008*, which outlines incident communications on a more tactical level than explored in this document.

In: Risk Management ...
Editor: Gustav Knudsen

ISBN: 978-1-62618-701-6

Chapter 3

CHEMICAL, BIOLOGICAL, RADIOLOGICAL, AND NUCLEAR RISK ASSESSMENTS: DHS SHOULD ESTABLISH MORE SPECIFIC GUIDANCE FOR THEIR USE*

United States Government Accountability Office

WHY GAO DID THIS STUDY

The 2001 anthrax attacks in the United States highlighted the need to develop response plans and capabilities to protect U.S. citizens from chemical, biological, radiological, and nuclear (CBRN) agents. Since 2004, the Department of Homeland Security (DHS) has spent at least $70 million developing more than 20 CBRN risk assessments. GAO was requested to assess, from fiscal year 2004 to the present, the extent to which DHS has used its CBRN risk assessments to inform CBRN response plans and CBRN capabilities, and has institutionalized their use. GAO examined relevant laws, Homeland Security Presidential Directives, an Executive Order, DHS guidance, and all 12 relevant interagency CBRN response plans developed by DHS. Based on a review of a United States governmentwide CBRN database and DHS interviews, among other things, GAO selected a nongeneralizable set

---

* This is an edited, reformatted and augmented version of United States Government Accountability Office, Publication No. GAO-12-272, dated January 2012.

of seven DHS capabilities used specifically for detecting or responding to CBRN incidents to identify examples of DHS's use of its CBRN risk assessments. GAO also interviewed relevant DHS officials. This is a public version of a classified report that GAO issued in October 2011. Information DHS deemed sensitive or classified has been redacted.

What GAO Recommends

GAO recommends that DHS develop more specific guidance, including written procedures, that details when and how DHS components should consider using the department's CBRN risk assessments to inform related response planning efforts and capability investment decision making. DHS agreed with the recommendation.

What GAO Found

Since 2004, DHS's use of its CBRN risk assessments to inform its CBRN response plans has varied, from directly influencing information in the plans to not being used at all. DHS guidance states that response planning and resource decisions should be informed by risk information. GAO's analysis showed that DHS used its CBRN risk assessments to directly inform 2 of 12 CBRN response plans GAO identified because planners considered the risk assessments to be more accurate than earlier DHS planning assumptions. For another 7 of the 12 plans, DHS officials said that the assessments indirectly informed the plans by providing background information prior to plan development. However, GAO could not independently verify this because DHS officials could not document how the risk assessments influenced the information contained in the plans. GAO's analysis found general consistency between the risk assessments and the plans. For the remaining 3 plans, DHS officials did not use the risk assessments to inform the plans; for 2 of the 3 plans DHS officials told GAO they were not aware of the assessments. DHS officials also noted that there was no departmental guidance on when or how the CBRN risk assessments should be used when developing such plans.

Since 2004, DHS's use of its CBRN risk assessments to inform its CBRN-specific capabilities has varied, from directly impacting its capabilities to not being used at all. Of the 7 capabilities GAO reviewed, one was directly informed by the risk assessments; DHS used its biological agent risk assessments to confirm that its BioWatch program could generally detect the biological agents posing the greatest risk. For 5 of the 7 capabilities, DHS officials said they used the risk assessments along with other information sources to partially inform these capabilities. For example, DHS used its chemical agent risk assessments to determine whether its chemical detectors and the risk assessments were generally aligned for the highest risk agents. For 3 of these 5 capabilities, GAO could not independently verify that they were partially informed by the risk assessments because DHS officials could not document how the risk assessments influenced the capabilities. DHS did not use its CBRN risk assessments to inform the remaining CBRN capability because the assessments were not needed to meet the capability's mission.

DHS and its components do not have written procedures to institutionalize their use of DHS's CBRN risk assessments for CBRN response planning and capability investment decisions. Standards for internal control in the federal government call for written procedures to better ensure management's directives are enforced. DHS does not have procedures that stipulate when and how DHS officials should use the department's CBRN risk assessments to inform CBRN response planning and capability investment decisions, and GAO found variation in the extent to which they were used. DHS officials agree with GAO that without written procedures, the consistent use of the department's CBRN risk assessments by DHS officials may not be ensured beyond the tenure of any given agency official. DHS could better help to ensure that its CBRN response plans and capabilities are consistently informed by the department's CBRN risk assessments by establishing written procedures detailing when and how DHS officials should consider using the risk assessments to inform their activities.

ABBREVIATIONS

BTRA	Biological Terrorism Risk Assessment
CBRN	Chemical, biological, radiological, and nuclear
CFO's PAE	DHS Office of the Chief Financial Officer's Program Analysis and Evaluations unit
CONPLAN	Concept of Operations Plan
CTRA	Chemical Terrorism Risk Assessment
CSAC	Chemical Security Analysis Center
DHS	Department of Homeland Security

DNDO	Domestic Nuclear Detection Office
Executive Order 13527	Executive Order 13527 – Establishing Federal Capability for the Timely Provision of Medical Countermeasures Following a Biological Attack
FEMA	Federal Emergency Management Agency
FOUO	For Official Use Only
HHS	Department of Health and Human Services
HSPD 8 Annex I	Homeland Security Presidential Directive 8 – National Preparedness, Annex I – National Planning
IND	Improvised Nuclear Device
IPS	Integrated Planning System
ITRA	Integrated CBRN Terrorism Risk Assessment
MTA	Material Threat Assessment
NBFAC	National Bioforensic Analysis Center
NBIC	National Biosurveillance Integration Center
NPG	National Preparedness Guidelines
NIRT	Nuclear Incident Response Teams
NPPD's RMA	DHS National Protection and Programs Directorate's Office of Risk Management and Analysis
NPS	National Planning Scenario
NRF	National Response Framework
NRP	National Response Plan
NTNFC	National Technical Nuclear Forensics Center
OHA	DHS Office of Health Affairs
OPLAN	Operational Plan
OPS	DHS Office of Operations Coordination
PPD 8	Presidential Policy Directive 8 – National Preparedness
POLICY	DHS Office of Policy
RDCDS	Rapidly Deployable Chemical Detection System
RDD	Radiological Dispersal Device
R/NTRA	Radiological and Nuclear Terrorism Risk Assessment
S&T	DHS Science and Technology Directorate
SGS	Strategic Guidance Statement
STRATPLAN	Strategic Plan
TRA	Terrorism Risk Assessment

January 25, 2012
The Honorable Joseph I. Lieberman
Chairman

The Honorable Susan M. Collins
Ranking Member
Committee on Homeland Security and
Governmental Affairs
United States Senate

The anthrax attacks of 2001 raised concerns that the United States is vulnerable to threats from chemical, biological, radiological, and nuclear (CBRN) agents. Moreover, the 2007 *National Strategy for Homeland Security* stated that terrorists have declared their intention to acquire and use CBRN agents as weapons to inflict catastrophic attacks against the United States.[1] More recently, the May 2010 *National Security Strategy* noted that the American people face no greater or more urgent danger than a terrorist attack with a nuclear weapon. The strategy further said that the effective dissemination of a lethal biological agent within a U.S. city would endanger the lives of hundreds of thousands of people and have unprecedented economic, societal, and political consequences.[2] In addition, multiple stakeholders have assessed the federal government's ability to protect the nation from CBRN agents and deemed it inadequate. For example, in January 2010, the congressionally mandated Commission on the Prevention of Weapons of Mass Destruction Proliferation and Terrorism reported that the federal government lacked the capability to rapidly recognize, respond to, and recover from a terrorist attack using biological agents.

Because CBRN agents differ in their potential to be used to cause widespread illness and death, members of Congress have expressed the need for the Department of Homeland Security (DHS) to assess the risks posed by CBRN agents to identify those that are highest risk and develop necessary response plans and capabilities.[3] To address these needs, DHS produces CBRN threat and risk assessments that analyze the potential for adverse outcomes as a result of an attack with such agents. Since 2004, DHS has spent over $70 million developing these analyses. Assessing the risks posed by CBRN agents requires analyzing and modeling areas of uncertainty, including determining an adversary's capability to acquire these agents, develop them into weapons, and disseminate them to estimate the plausibility and consequences of such attacks. These assessments are designed so that decision makers can use them to inform priorities, develop or compare courses of action, and inform federal planning and investments for responding to the highest risk CBRN incidents.

The 2007 National Strategy for Homeland Security (Strategy) notes that the nation must apply a risk-based framework across all homeland security efforts to identify and assess potential hazards, determine what levels of relative risk are acceptable, and prioritize and allocate resources among homeland security partners to, among other things, respond to and recover from CBRN incidents. The Strategy states that a disciplined approach to managing risk will help to achieve overall effectiveness and efficiency in securing the nation. Further, the Strategy notes that for homeland security efforts to succeed federal dollars must be allocated based on risk assessments and on accountability for results; once allocated, funds must be used to support or develop operational plans and their derivative requirements and capabilities.

In June 2011 we reported on DHS and the Department of Health and Human Services (HHS) coordination for developing CBRN risk assessments.[4] We found that DHS and HHS have coordinated with each other and with other federal departments to varying extents over time to develop CBRN risk assessments, but that neither department has written procedures for developing these assessments. We recommended that DHS develop time frames and milestones to better ensure timely development of and interagency agreement on written procedures for the development of its CBRN risk assessments, and DHS agreed with our recommendation. DHS stated that the department had begun efforts to develop milestones and time frames for development of strategic and implementation plans for interagency CBRN risk assessment development.

You asked us to examine DHS's use of its CBRN risk assessments. This report assesses the extent to which, from 2004 to the present, DHS (1) used its CBRN risk assessments to inform its CBRN response plans and (2) CBRN capabilities, and (3) institutionalized the use of its CBRN risk assessments for such activities through written policies and procedures.

This report is a public version of the prior classified report that we provided to you. DHS deemed some of the information in the prior report as sensitive or classified, which must be protected from public disclosure. Therefore, this report omits sensitive or classified information contained in DHS's CBRN risk assessments and CBRN response plans. In addition, this report omits sensitive or classified information about DHS CBRN capabilities. Although the information provided in this report is more limited in scope, it addresses the same objectives as the classified report. Also, the overall methodology used for both reports is the same.

To address objectives 1 and 2, we analyzed relevant federal laws, presidential directives, executive orders, and national strategies. For example, we reviewed presidential directives on national preparedness and CBRN-related activities and an executive order on the distribution of medical countermeasures in the event of a domestic biological attack. We analyzed these documents to identify requirements for DHS to develop CBRN risk assessments as well as interagency CBRN-specific response plans and capabilities, and for any criteria contained within these documents to guide the use of DHS's CBRN risk assessments to inform response planning activities and capability program management. We analyzed the CBRN risk assessments, response plans, and documents on the capabilities DHS has developed since 2004—the year initial legislative requirements were enacted for the department to develop the assessments—to determine the contents of these assessments and these plans. For the purposes of this report, we consider DHS's CBRN risk assessments to include its Terrorism Risk Assessments (TRAs) and Material Threat Assessments (MTAs).[5]

We analyzed all 12 CBRN-specific interagency response plans developed by DHS that are designed for responding to CBRN incidents to determine the extent to which they identify DHS's CBRN risk assessments as a source of information contained within the plans.[6] We also asked DHS officials to provide us with documentation showing how specific information from the risk assessments, if any, was incorporated into the plans. We then reviewed the response plans to identify CBRN agent-specific planning assumptions contained within the plans. We selected assumptions that contained information about the unique features of the CBRN agent, the threat, the attack scenario, DHS's ability to detect the agent and respond, public health consequences of an attack, or time frames for response. We excluded generic statements regarding coordination of the federal response to an attack and the roles and responsibilities of relevant agencies because the CBRN risk assessments do not assess these topics. We compared these assumptions to the information contained in the risk assessments to determine the relative level of consistency between examples of this type of information contained in the plans and in the assessments.[7] Our analysis did not compare all assumptions in the plans, including those that were nonCBRN agent specific, to all the assumptions in the risk assessments.

Further, we identified a nongeneralizable set of seven CBRN-specific capabilities by interviewing DHS component program officials and conducting a search of a Department of Defense database that contains a listing of U.S. governmentwide CBRN capabilities and activities. We used these interviews and the database to limit our scope to capabilities that are specifically deployed and are being used by DHS components to prevent, detect, and respond to CBRN incidents. We did not include within our scope capabilities for responding to all-hazards that may also be used for responding to CBRN incidents, nor did we include, among others, capabilities related to intelligence, law enforcement, training, or research and development. We reviewed documentation of these programs to determine the extent to which they are informed by DHS's CBRN risk assessments. When possible, we directly compared the lists of threat agents that are addressed by the capabilities to the relevant lists of high-risk agents identified in the CBRN risk assessments. We did not compare any other information in the CBRN risk assessments—such as assumptions about U.S. vulnerabilities to specific threat agents or attack consequences—to the capabilities.

We also interviewed officials from DHS offices, components, and agencies to obtain information on whether and how they used the TRAs and MTAs in developing a given response plan or developing and managing a given capability. Specifically, we interviewed DHS officials from DHS's:

- Science and Technology Directorate (S&T),
- Office of the Chief Financial Officer (CFO), Program Analysis and Evaluations (PA&E),
- Office of Health Affairs (OHA),
- Office of Operations Coordination (OPS),
- Office of Policy (POLICY),
- National Protection and Programs Directorate's (NPPD) Office of Risk Management and Analysis (RMA),
- Domestic Nuclear Detection Office (DNDO), and
- Federal Emergency Management Agency (FEMA).

To address the third objective, we analyzed *Standards for Internal Control in the Federal Government* for guidelines on internal controls.[8] We then obtained written policies or procedures developed by DHS offices, components, or agencies that describe whether and how DHS's CBRN risk assessments should be used when DHS officials develop CBRN response plans or capabilities. We compared the standards for internal control against the status of DHS's development of policies and procedures for using its CBRN risk assessments to inform its plans and capabilities. We also interviewed DHS officials to obtain information on the reasons why DHS has or has not institutionalized use of the TRAs and MTAs through written policies and procedures.

We conducted this performance audit from February through December 2011 in accordance with generally accepted government auditing standards. Those standards require that we plan and perform the audit to obtain sufficient, appropriate evidence to provide a reasonable basis for our findings and conclusions based on our audit objectives. We believe that the evidence obtained provides a reasonable basis for our findings and conclusions based on our audit objectives.

BACKGROUND

Multiple DHS offices, components, and agencies have roles and responsibilities in DHS's development of CBRN risk assessments, response plans, and capabilities. Specifically:

- S&T is responsible for the development of DHS's CBRN risk assessments—the TRAs and MTAs.
- CFO's PA&E unit is responsible for developing resource allocation decisions for capability investments through DHS's Planning, Programming, Budgeting and Execution system.
- OHA is responsible for leading DHS's biological and chemical defense activities and provides medical and public health expertise to support the department's efforts.
- OPS is responsible for coordinating DHS's operational activities for incident response, including for CBRN incidents.
- POLICY is responsible for advising the Secretary of Homeland Security in the development of DHS's policies for CBRN plans and capabilities.
- NPPD's RMA is responsible for leading DHS's approach to risk management and the application of risk information to departmental activities.
- DNDO is responsible for domestic radiological and nuclear detection efforts and integration of federal nuclear forensics programs.
- FEMA is responsible for leading the nation's effort for preparing to respond to emergencies and disasters.

DHS Risk Management

DHS engages in risk management activities to help ensure the nation's ability to protect against and respond to incidents using CBRN agents.[9] DHS's Risk Lexicon provides the following definitions for risk-related terms:[10]

- Risk—potential for an adverse outcome assessed as a function of threats, vulnerabilities, and consequences associated with an incident, event, or occurrence.
- Risk Assessment—product or process which collects information and assigns values to risks for the purpose of informing priorities, developing or comparing courses of action, and informing decision making.
- Risk Management—process of identifying, analyzing, assessing, and communicating risk and accepting, avoiding, transferring, or controlling it to an acceptable level considering associated costs and benefits of any actions taken.

The department's 2010 *Quadrennial Homeland Security Review* notes the importance of incorporating information from risk assessments into departmental decision making, one aspect of the department's homeland security risk management process.[11] According to DHS doctrine, risk management applications include the use of risk information to inform, among others, strategic and operational planning and resource decisions. This report focuses on DHS's use of the third step of its risk management process—risk assessment—and the application of risk assessment results to inform CBRN response plans and capabilities. DHS notes that risk information is usually one of many factors—not necessarily the sole factor—that decision makers consider when deciding which strategies to pursue for managing risk. These additional factors may include strategic and political considerations, among others. See figure 1 for a graphic depiction of DHS's risk management process.

DHS's CBRN Risk Assessments

DHS is responsible for assessing the risks posed by various CBRN agents, as directed by the Project BioShield Act of 2004[12] and Homeland Security Presidential Directives 10 – Biodefense for the 21st Century, 18 – *Medical*

Countermeasures against Weapons of Mass Destruction, and 22 – *National Domestic Chemical Defense*. To this end, S&T develops CBRN TRAs and MTAs.[13]

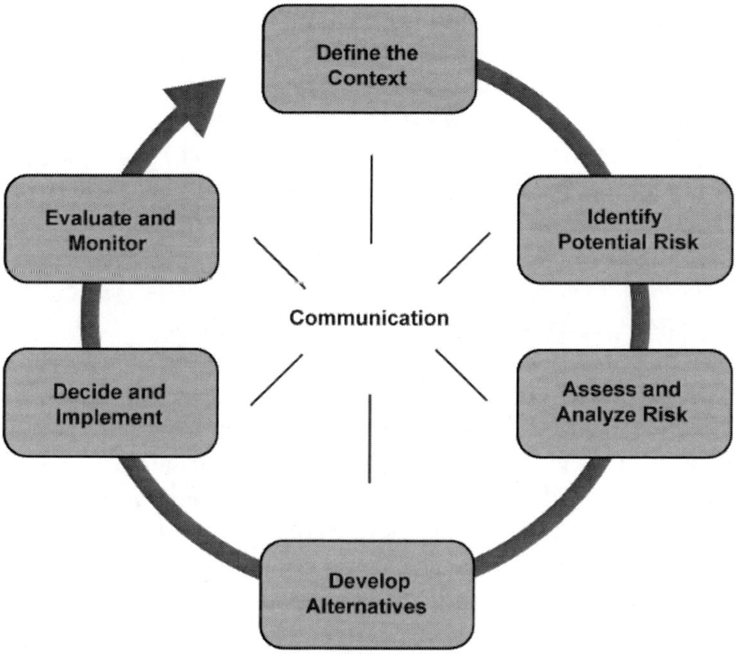

Source: DHS Risk Management Fundamentals.

Figure 1. DHS's Risk Management Process.

Each TRA assesses the relative risks posed by multiple CBRN agents based on variable threats, vulnerabilities, and consequences. Since 2006, DHS has developed eight TRA reports:

- Biological Terrorism Risk Assessments (BTRA) in 2006, 2008, and 2010;
- Chemical Terrorism Risk Assessments (CTRA) in 2008 and 2010;
- Radiological/Nuclear Terrorism Risk Assessment (R/NTRA) in 2011; and
- Integrated CBRN Terrorism Risk Assessments (ITRA) in 2008 and 2011.

Each MTA assesses the threat posed by a given, individual CBRN agent or class of agents and the potential number of human exposures in plausible, high-consequence scenarios. Since 2004, DHS has developed 17 MTA reports. DHS uses the MTAs to determine which CBRN agents pose a material threat sufficient to affect national security.[14]

The Project BioShield Act describes specific ways in which the MTAs may be used in efforts to procure certain medical countermeasures.[15] However, the various presidential directives note that while the TRAs may be used to inform decision making, they are not specific as to when or how these risk assessments should be used by DHS officials to inform CBRN response planning or capability investments.

DHS's CBRN Response Plans and Capabilities

(U) We identified CBRN-specific interagency response plans among three families of interagency plans developed by DHS that are designed for responding to CBRN incidents. These families of plans include plans developed under (1) Executive Order 13527 – Establishing Federal Capability for the Timely Provision of Medical Countermeasures Following a Biological Attack (Executive Order 13527) and (2) Homeland Security Presidential Directive 8 Annex I – National Planning (HSPD 8 Annex I), and as a part of (3) the National Response Framework's (NRF) CBRN-specific incident annexes.16,17 See table 1 for a listing of the 12 plans we reviewed.

Presidential Policy Directive 8 – National Preparedness, issued in March 2011, superseded HSPD 8 Annex I and its requirement for SGS, STRATPLANs, CONPLANs, and OPLANS to be developed for each NPS.[18] In May 2011 DHS issued an implementation plan for the new directive which calls for DHS to develop an interagency operational plan to implement the NRF by September 2012. According to FEMA officials, this interagency operational plan may include a range of incident annexes, potentially including annexes specific to CBRN incidents. This operational plan and related annexes have yet to be developed.

We selected seven CBRN-specific capabilities managed by DHS that are designed to prevent, detect, or respond to CBRN incidents to assess the extent to which these capabilities are informed by DHS's CBRN risk assessments. These seven capabilities are managed by various DHS components, including OHA, S&T, FEMA, and DNDO. Table 2 provides a listing of the DHS CBRN capabilities we analyzed and a description of each program.

Table 1. DHS's CBRN-specific Interagency Response Plans Reviewed

Response plan family	CBRN-specific response plan[a]
Executive Order 13527 – Establishing Federal Capability for the Timely Provision of Medical Countermeasures Following a Biological Attack (related plans issued in 2010)	
In response to requirements in Executive Order 13527, DHS developed three plans in coordination with its interagency partners that are designed to reduce the potential for large numbers of casualties and fatalities in the United States following a geographically dispersed biological attack. These plans were developed to address a range of activities necessary for responding to such incidents.	U.S. Postal Service Medical Countermeasure Dispensing Model and Annex on Law Enforcement Support to the Postal Model Operational Concepts and Requirements for a Federal Medical Countermeasures Rapid Response and related Federal Interagency Operational Plan: Rapid Medical Countermeasure Dispensing Plan for the Provision of Medical Countermeasures to EnsureContinuity of Federal Mission Essential Functions
Homeland Security Presidential Directive 8 Annex I – National Planning (related plans issued 2008-2009)	
HSPD-8 Annex I called for the development of a standardized federal planning process—the Integrated Planning System (IPS)—and a family of response plans using IPS and the National Planning Scenarios (NPS), including strategic guidance statements (SGS), strategic plans (STRATPLANS), concepts of operation plans (CONPLANS), and operations plans (OPLANS).[b]One SGS and three STRATPLANS (with related annexes) were developed under IPS for the CBRN-specific NPS prior to this effort being put on an indefinite hold in July 2009 by the White House National Security Staff pending the revision of HSPD 8.[c]Presidential Policy Directive 8 – National Preparedness(PPD 8) superseded HSPD 8 Annex I and its provisions on March 30, 2011.[d]	SGS for Chemical Attacks STRATPLAN for Biological Attacks[e] • Annex A: Aerosol Anthrax • Annex B: Plague • Annex C: Food Contamination • Annex D: Foot and Mouth Disease STRATPLAN for Terrorist Use of Radiological Dispersal Devices STRATPLAN for Terrorist Use of an Improvised Nuclear Device
National Response Framework (related annexes originally issued in 2004 and reissued in 2008)	
Developed by FEMA and issued by DHS, the NRF is the doctrine that guides how federal, state, local, and tribal governments, along with nongovernmental and private sector entities, will collectively respond to and recover from all-hazards including CBRN incidents. The NRF includes, among others, seven Incident Annexes which are to address aspects of how the United States responds to specific types of incidents. Two of these incident annexes are for CBRN events.	Biological Incident Annex Nuclear/Radiological Incident Annex

Source: GAO analysis of presidential and DHS documents.

[a]For the purposes of this report, in addition to stand-alone plans, we also refer to CBRN-specific annexes as "plans."

[b]DHS, National Planning Scenarios (Washington, D.C.: April 2005). The NPS establish common assumptions regarding potential vulnerabilities and consequences posed by plausible, high-consequence natural disasters and terrorist incidents, including attacks with CBRN agents, to guide emergency response planning nationwide.

[c]For the purposes of this report, we reviewed the most detailed response plan developed under HSPD 8 Annex I for a given CBRN agent. Specifically, if an SGS was developed but a related STRATPLAN had not been, we analyzed the SGS for the given agent. If a STRATPLAN had been developed, but a related CONPLAN had not been, we analyzed the STRATPLAN for the given agent. Although a CONPLAN for responding to an improvised nuclear device (IND) was issued by DHS in an interim format in November 2009, we only reviewed the IND STRATPLAN because it was the most detailed finalized plan produced.

[d]PPD 8 states that plans developed under HSPD 8 Annex I remain in effect until rescinded. The implementation plan for PPD 8, issued in May 2011, directs DHS to develop national planning frameworks for the prevention, protection, mitigation, response, and recovery mission areas by June 30, 2012, and related interagency operational plans for each of these frameworks by September 25, 2012. The implementation plan notes that the frameworks are intended to align key roles and responsibilities for the delivery of necessary capabilities for each mission area. The implementation plan also notes that the related interagency operational plans for each mission area are to support the various frameworks and describe the concept of operations for integrating and synchronizing existing national level capabilities to support federal, state, local, tribal, and territorial plans.

[e]For the purposes of this report we consider the STRATPLAN for Biological Attacks to count as four plans because it contains four agent- or incident-specific annexes. We reviewed each annex as if it were a stand-alone plan.

Table 2. Select DHS CBRN-specific Capabilities Reviewed

Capability and DHS component	Description of capability
Select chemical capabilities	
Rapidly Deployable Chemical Detection System (RDCDS) *OHA*	The RDCDS is a mobile set of chemical detectors that can be deployed across the nation and set up prior to large public events. The RDCDS detectors can be programmed to detect specific chemical threat agents and in the event of an attack, the detectors are intended to enable federal, state, and local officials to quickly identify the agent and respond.
Chemical Security Analysis Center (CSAC) *S&T*	The CSAC works to provide a scientific basis for understanding the risks posed by chemical threat agents and for attribution associated with their use in a terrorist attack. The CSAC is a resource that provides a centralized compilation of chemical hazard data, using these data to assess chemical threats through risk assessments and other products.

Capability and DHS component	Description of capability
Select biological capabilities	
BioWatch *OHA*	BioWatch is a federally managed, locally operated biosurveillance system of air sample collectors designed to detect the release of select aerosolized bioterrorism agents. In the event of such a release, BioWatch is intended to enable federal, state, and local officials to identify the agent and respond.
National Bioforensic Analysis Center (NBFAC) *S&T*	The NBFAC conducts bioforensic analysis of evidence from a biocrime or terrorist attack to attain a "biological fingerprint" to help investigators identify perpetrators and determine the origin and method of attack. The NBFAC is designated by Homeland Security Presidential Directive 10 – *Biodefense for the 21stCentury*to be the lead federal facility to conduct and facilitate the technical forensic analysis and interpretation of materials recovered following a biological attack in support of the appropriate lead federal agency.
National Biosurveillance Integration Center *OHA*	The NBIC works to integrate and analyze information from biosurveillance systems acrossthe federal government, and to disseminate alerts if any biological events are detected.
Select radiological and nuclear capabilities	
Nuclear Incident Response Teams (NIRT) *FEMA*	The NIRTs are specialized teams managed day to day by the Department of Energy's National Nuclear Security Administration and the Environmental Protection Agency. In theevent of a high-consequence nuclear incident, the NIRTs fall under FEMA's operational control. FEMA works to provide expert technical advice and support in disaster response operations and other needs involving nuclear weapons accidents, radiological accidents, lost or stolen nuclear material incidents, and acts of nuclear terrorism.
National Technical Nuclear Forensics Center (NTNFC) *DNDO*	The NTNFC has two primary missions. The first is to provide centralized planning, integration, and stewardship of the nation's nuclear forensics activities to ensure a ready, robust, and enduring capability in coordination with other federal departments and agencies. The second is to advance technical capabilities in the area of predetonation forensics for radiological and nuclear materials.

Source: GAO analysis of DHS documents and information provided by DHS officials.

DHS Used Its CBRN Risk Assessments to Directly or Indirectly Inform 9 of 12 of Its CBRN Response Plans

Since the first DHS CBRN risk assessments were developed in 2004, DHS used the risk assessments to varying degrees to directly or indirectly inform development of 9 of the 12 CBRN-specific response plans we identified.[19] Our analysis showed that 2 of the 12 plans were directly informed by the risk assessments, while DHS officials told us that 7 of the 12 plans were indirectly informed by the risk assessments. However, we could not independently verify this for these 7 plans because DHS officials could not document how the risk assessments influenced information contained in the plans. Three of the response plans were not informed by the risk assessments, according to DHS officials. Our analysis of a limited set of planning assumptions in the plans compared to information contained in the risk assessments showed general consistency between the plans and the risk assessments. DHS's guidelines state that response plans should be informed by risk assessment information to supplement risk-related information contained in the National Planning Scenarios (NPS) used for developing emergency response plans.[20,21] DHS's 2009 Integrated Planning System (IPS) also identifies risk assessments as one source of information that should be used to inform response plan development.[22] This guidance, however, does not define what it means for response plans to be informed by risk assessments or how planners should use specific types of risk assessments, such as DHS's TRAs and MTAs, when developing or revising related plans. Of the 12 CBRN response plans developed by DHS that we reviewed, none of the plans were developed solely in response to a given CBRN threat agent being identified as high risk in DHS's CBRN risk assessments. Rather, these plans were developed in response to requirements in an executive order and as part of families of plans developed in response to provisions in presidential directives.[23] See table 3 for a list of the CBRN response plans and whether each plan was directly, indirectly, or not informed by DHS's CBRN risk assessments during its development.

Table 3. Extent to Which DHS's CBRN Risk Assessments Informed Development of its CBRN Response Plans

Response plan-family	CBRN response plan[a]	Informed by DHS's CBRN riskassessmentsc
Executive Order 13527 – Establishing Federal Capability for the Timely Provision of Medical Countermeasures Following a Biological Attack (related plans issued in 2010)	U.S. Postal Service Medical Countermeasure Dispensing Model and Annex on Law Enforcement Support to the Postal Model	Indirectly
	Operational Concepts and Requirements for a Federal Medical Countermeasures Rapid Response and related Federal	Indirectly

Response plan-family	CBRN response plana	Informed by DHS's CBRN riskassessmentsc
	Interagency Operational Plan: Rapid Medical Countermeasure Dispensing	
	Plan for the Provision of Medical Countermeasures to Ensure Continuity of Federal Mission Essential Functions	Indirectly
Homeland Security Presidential Directive 8 Annex I – National Planning (related plans issued 2008-2009)	SGS for Chemical Attacks	Indirectly
	STRATPLAN for Biological Attacks[b]	
	•Annex A: Aerosol Anthrax	Directly
	•Annex B: Plague	Directly
	•Annex C: Food Contamination	Indirectly
	•Annex D: Foot and Mouth Disease	No
	STRATPLAN for Terrorist Use of Radiological Dispersal Devices	Indirectly
	STRATPLAN for Terrorist Use of an Improvised Nuclear Device	Indirectly
National Response Framework (related annexes originally issued in 2004 and reissued in 2008)	Biological Incident Annex	No
	Nuclear/Radiological Incident Annex	No

Source: GAO analysis of presidential and DHS documents and information provided by DHS officials.

[a]For the purposes of this report, in addition to stand-alone plans, we refer to CBRN-specific annexes as "plans."

[b]For the purposes of this report we consider the STRATPLAN for Biological Attacks to count as four plans because it contains four agent- or incident-specific annexes. We reviewed each annex as if it were a stand-alone plan.

[c]For the purposes of this report, we identify a response plan as being directly informed by DHS's CBRN risk assessments if the plan specifically identifies the TRAs or MTAs as a source for information contained within the plan, or if DHS officials were able to provide documentation showing how specific information from the risk assessments was incorporated into the plan.

We identify a response plan as being indirectly informed by DHS's CBRN risk assessments if DHS officials said that the TRAs or MTAs served as a source of background information that was known to officials involved in the development of the plans, but the plans do not specifically identify the risk assessments as a source for information contained in the plans and DHS officials were unable to provide documentation showing their use.

All Three Biological Response Plans Developed under Executive Order 13527 Were Indirectly Informed by DHS's CBRN Risk Assessments

The three biological response plans developed in response to Executive Order 13527 were indirectly informed by DHS's CBRN risk assessments, according to DHS officials, but officials could not provide documentation showing how the risk assessments influenced the development of these plans. The plans developed under this order are designed to implement the administration's policy of preparing for the timely provision of medical countermeasures to the American people in the event of a biological attack—in particular an aerosolized anthrax attack—to mitigate potential illnesses and deaths.

According to officials from OHA—which led development of all three plans for DHS—both the BTRA and anthrax MTA were used to help educate planners prior to the development of the plans.[24] The BTRA and anthrax MTA were used, according to OHA officials, because they provided planners with scientifically-based information on the threat, vulnerabilities, and consequences posed by an aerosolized anthrax attack. OHA officials said that this helped inform initial discussions in the interagency workgroups that were responsible for developing the plans.

OHA planners stated that the BTRA served as a source of background information on the risk posed by anthrax relative to other biological agents. The planners also said they used the 2005 anthrax MTA and a 2008 unclassified version of the anthrax MTA to help understand the specific planning assumptions that would need to be addressed by the three plans. [25] OHA officials said they used these MTAs because the anthrax MTAs provide more up-to-date and accurate information on the exposures and potential casualties that would occur during an anthrax attack than is provided in the 2005 anthrax NPS. As a result, according to DHS officials, these plans were better informed than they would have been had the anthrax NPS been the sole source of background information used to develop the plans.

DHS officials could not produce documentation showing how the BTRA and the anthrax MTAs influenced the development of these plans. As a result, we could not independently verify that the risk assessments were used by DHS officials to influence development of the plans. Our analysis of a limited set of planning assumptions in the plans compared to information contained in the DHS CBRN risk assessments showed general consistency between the information contained in the plans and the information contained in the risk assessments.[26]

DHS officials emphasized that the DHS CBRN risk assessments are just one source of data among many that DHS planners used in the course of their planning activities under the executive order. According to officials, additional sources of information included, among others, current intelligence information, emerging scientific research on CBRN threat agents, and the subject matter expertise of officials from DHS, HHS, DOD, and others who were involved in the development of the plans.

Six of the Seven CBRN Response Plans Developed under HSPD-8 Annex I Were Directly or Indirectly Informed by DHS's CBRN Risk Assessments

Our analysis showed that two of the seven CBRN response plans developed under HSPD 8 Annex I—the anthrax and plague annexes— were directly informed by DHS's CBRN risk assessments. Four of the seven plans were indirectly informed by the risk assessments, according to DHS officials: the SGS for chemical attacks, STRATPLANs for radiological and nuclear device attacks, and the food contamination annex. However, officials could not provide documentation showing how the risk assessments influenced the development of these plans. As a result, we could not independently verify that the risk assessments were used by DHS officials to influence development of the plans. The last plan—the foot and mouth disease annex—was not informed by the risk assessments. The seven plans were created to address provisions in HSPD 8 Annex I that called for the establishment of a family of plans that were to be developed for each NPS to enhance national preparedness.[27,28] IPS, which was developed as directed by Annex I, was designed to establish a standardized approach to federal planning. IPS states that planners should use risk assessments as one source of information to inform the development of response plans.[29]

According to officials from OPS—which served as the lead for the interagency team that developed the plans—DHS's TRAs and MTAs were used to either directly or indirectly inform all but one of the plans. OPS officials noted that they were briefed on the contents of the TRAs to understand the relative risks posed by various CBRN threat agents in the course of collecting background information to inform their planning efforts. OPS officials also reviewed the MTAs during their background research, which they said were useful because they provided specific planning assumptions for plausible, high-consequence attacks using such agents. Specifically, OPS used:

- the anthrax and plague MTAs to directly inform development of the anthrax and plague annexes issued in May 2009,[30]
- the 2008 CTRA and various chemical MTAs to indirectly inform development of the Chemical Attack SGS issued in June 2009,[31]
- the Nuclear/Radiological Appendix to the 2008 Integrated CBRN TRA (ITRA) and radiological and nuclear agent MTA to indirectly inform development of the Radiological Dispersal and Improvised Nuclear Device STRATPLANS, and
- the 2008 BTRA, CTRA, and ITRA, as well as the various MTAs, to indirectly inform development of the food contamination annex issued in May 2009.

In two of seven plans, our analysis showed that OPS officials used DHS's CBRN risk assessments to directly inform the plans by modifying planning assumptions contained in the NPS with information obtained from the relevant MTA. OPS officials stated that when they developed the SGS and STRATPLANs, they started by using the planning assumptions from the relevant NPS, as called for in the National Preparedness Guidelines (NPG) and IPS. OPS then used the anthrax and plague MTAs to modify the exposure and casualty estimates for the anthrax and plague annexes. According to OPS officials, they used these MTAs because the information on the consequences of such attacks was more accurate and up to date than the information contained in the NPS.

In four of seven plans, according to OPS officials, the plans were indirectly informed by the planners' knowledge of information contained in the TRAs and MTAs. OPS officials stated that the relevant TRAs and MTAs indirectly informed their planning activities for the Chemical SGS, Radiological Dispersal and Improvised Nuclear Device STRATPLANs, and food contamination annex. OPS officials said that a range of interagency planners involved in the development of these plans, such as officials from OHA and HHS, were knowledgeable about DHS's CBRN risk assessments and would therefore have indirectly incorporated this information when drafting the plans.

One plan—the foot and mouth disease annex—was not informed by the TRAs or MTAs, according to OPS officials, because DHS's CBRN risk assessments primarily focus on consequences to human health whereas this annex focuses on a foreign animal disease with no significant human health effects. According to officials, this annex was instead based on planning assumptions contained in its associated NPS, as called for by HSPD 8 Annex I, in addition to recommendations from officials with relevant subject matter expertise from the U.S. Department of Agriculture.[32]

Our analysis of a limited set of planning assumptions in the HSPD 8 Annex I plans compared to information contained in the DHS CBRN risk assessments showed that they are generally consistent. [33]

However, as previously noted, DHS officials emphasized that the DHS CBRN risk assessments are just one source of data among many that DHS planners utilize in the course of their planning activities.

Neither CBRN Response Plan Developed as Part of the National Response Framework Was Informed by DHS's CBRN Risk Assessments

Neither of the CBRN response plans developed as part of the NRF—the Biological or Nuclear/Radiological Incident Annexes—were informed by DHS's CBRN risk assessments, according to FEMA officials.[34] The NRF was developed to provide the structure and mechanisms for federal support to state and local incident managers for domestic all-hazard events, as called for in Homeland Security Presidential Directive 5 – Management of Domestic Incidents. DHS's Interim National Preparedness Goal of 2005 and related NPG of 2007 state that DHS response plans should incorporate risk assessments. However, according to FEMA officials, the TRAs and MTAs were not used when they revised the Biological and Nuclear/Radiological Incident Annexes.

FEMA officials provided multiple reasons for this. First, they noted that these plans are updated versions of the same plans that were originally developed in 2004, before DHS first published its CBRN risk assessments.

Second, the FEMA planners responsible for overseeing revision efforts said that they had been unaware of DHS's CBRN risk assessments. Third, according to FEMA officials, even if the FEMA planners had been aware of the TRAs and MTAs, there was no departmental guidance on when or how the CBRN risk assessments should be used when developing such plans (this is discussed in the third objective of this report).

DHS Used Its CBRN Risk Assessments to Directly or Partially Inform Six of Seven of Its CBRN Capabilities

Since 2004, DHS's use of its CBRN risk assessments to inform its CBRN-specific capability investments has varied, from directly impacting its capabilities to not being used at all. Six of the seven CBRN capabilities we examined were informed by DHS's CBRN risk assessments to some extent, according to program officials, DHS documents, and our analysis (see table 4).[35] Our analysis showed that one of the seven capabilities was directly informed by the risk assessments, while our analysis showed or DHS officials told us that five of the seven capabilities were partially informed by the risk assessments. However, we could not independently verify this for three of these five capabilities because DHS officials could not document how the risk assessments influenced the capabilities. DHS has developed policies and guidance on the use of risk information for the department's activities, but DHS has not issued guidance to program managers that specifies when or how they should use the CBRN risk assessments to inform CBRN capabilities (this is discussed in the third objective of this report). The DHS Strategic Plan for 2008-2013 states that resource decisions should be informed by relevant risk assessments, but does not provide specific guidance on when or how such decisions should be informed by the department's CBRN risk assessments.[36] Additionally, the Secretary of Homeland Security's March 2011 Management Directive stated that DHS policy is to use risk information and analysis to inform decision making and instructs DHS components to establish mission-appropriate risk management capabilities.[37] See table 4 for a summary of the CBRN capabilities and whether each capability was directly, partially, or not informed by DHS's CBRN risk assessments.

Our analysis showed that the extent to which the CBRN capabilities we examined were informed by DHS's CBRN risk assessments varied, but DHS officials described reasons for this variance, as discussed below. In addition, DHS officials noted that basic scientific differences between chemical, biological, and radiological/nuclear threat agents and materials also provide explanations about the differences in how the CBRN risk assessments are used to inform capabilities. For example, DHS officials told us that the relative risk rankings amongst biological agents may be more meaningful than the ranking amongst radiological materials because there are greater differences associated with detecting biological agents, as well as their consequences.

Table 4. Extent to Which DHS's CBRN Risk Assessments Informed Select DHS CBRN-specific Capabilities

Capability and DHS component	Description of capability	Informed by DHS'sCBRN risk assessmentsa
Select chemical capabilities		
Rapidly Deployable Chemical Detection System (RDCDS) *OHA*	A mobile set of chemical air sample collectors designed to dectect chemical threat agents.	Partially
Chemical Security Analysis Center (CSAC) *S&T*	The CSAC works to provide a basis (1) for understanding the risks posed by chemical threat agents and (2) for attribution associated with their use in a terrorist attack.	Partially
Select biological capabilities		
BioWatch *OHA*	A mobile set of biological air sample collectors designed to detect biological threat agents.	Directly
National Bioforensic Analysis Center (NBFAC) *S&T*	The NBFAC conducts bioforensic analysis of evidence from a biocrime or terrorist attack to attain a "biological fingerprint" to assist investigations.	Partially
National Biosurveillance Integration Center (NBIC) *OHA*	The NBIC works to integrate and analyze information from biosurveillance systems across the federal government, and to disseminate alerts if any biological events are detected.	Partially
Select radiological and nuclear capabilities		
Nuclear Incident Response Teams (NIRT) *FEMA*	The NIRT teams are managed day to day by the Department of Energy and the Environmental Protection Agency. In the event of a high-consequence nuclear incident, the NIRTs fall under FEMA's operational control.	Partially
National Technical Nuclear Forensics Center (NTNFC) *DNDO*	The NTNFC works to advance technical capabilities in the area of predetonation forensics for radiological and nuclear materials and also works to ensure the long-term sustainability of this capability.	No

Source: GAO analysis of DHS documents and information provided by DHS officials.

[a]For the purposes of this report, we define directly informed to mean that program managers used the CBRN risk assessments to directly align the capability with the threat agents of significant concern and program managers provided us with documentation of these actions. We define partially informed to mean that program managers told us they used the CBRN risk assessments, as well as other information sources, to inform the development or implementation of the capability.

Select DHS Chemical Capabilities

DHS program managers used the risk assessments to partially inform the program management of the RDCDS and the CSAC, as described below. The Director of the CSAC told us that because there are over 13 million possible chemicals that could be considered threat agents, it is impossible to come up with a relative risk ranking of all the chemicals. Therefore, the results of the CTRA are designed to be representative of the highest risk chemical agents and used as a guide—not a definitive resource—for informing capability and planning decisions related to such agents. Additionally, certain chemical compounds have similar enough compositions to be considered together when developing capabilities and response plans.

Rapidly Deployable Chemical Detection System (RDCDS)

The OHA Chemical Defense Program used the CTRA to partially inform its RDCDS, according to our analysis as well as DHS officials and documentation. We compared the lists of threat agents that have been programmed to be detected by RDCDS detectors against chemical agents of significant concern in the 2008 and 2010 CTRAs and found that they were generally consistent.[38] The RDCDS program manager told us that the list of threat agents monitored by RDCDS has not changed since 2005 as DHS developed the first and second iterations of the CTRA. However, the program manager told us that when the first CTRA was issued in 2008, program officials reviewed its content to determine whether chemical agents of significant concern in the CTRA were aligned with the chemicals detected by RDCDS. The official said that based on this initial assessment, the RDCDS was generally aligned with the chemical agents of greatest concern.

Chemical Security Analysis Center (CSAC)

The Director of the CSAC told us that because a key CSAC mission is to develop the CTRA and the chemical MTAs, these risk assessments are used—to varying extents—to inform the other capabilities that the CSAC maintains. Other capabilities include providing 24/7 technical assistance to other DHS components that encounter possible chemical attack situations, such as the National Operations Center. According to the CSAC Director, information from the CTRA is included in the knowledge management system that is used in maintaining this technical assistance capability. However, the CSAC could not provide us with documentation of how it had used the CBRN risk assessments to inform this capability. Further, the CSAC Director told us that the CTRA also informs the CSAC's work in developing models for other DHS components on the effects of certain chemical incidents. We reviewed a CSAC study for the DHS Transportation Security Administration about the release of chemical gases into the atmosphere and found that in the study the CSAC had modeled releases of two different chemical agents, both of which are among the chemical agents of significant concern in the CTRA.

Select DHS Biological Capabilities

We analyzed the extent to which DHS officials used the BTRA and the biological MTAs to inform the program management of three capabilities—BioWatch, the NBFAC, and the NBIC. Our analysis showed that DHS program managers used the risk assessments to either directly inform (BioWatch) or partially inform (NBFAC and NBIC) their decisions, as described below. The program manager of BioWatch told us that it makes sense for the program to use the most reliable tool available to them—in this case, the CBRN risk assessments—to determine what agents to program into their detection system. The director of the NBFAC told us that the BTRA was used on one occasion to directly inform program management and prioritization. The NBIC branch chief told us that the BTRA is used at a strategic level and that the center's staff is very familiar with the contents of the BTRA and the biological MTAs. However, he stated that the NBIC's mission is to monitor detection efforts for all biological agents, particularly emerging infectious diseases, and to provide alerts about potentially dangerous biological incidents to state and local homeland security professionals. Therefore, the NBIC branch chief said that the relative risk ranking of a given biological agent would not be an appropriate basis for the prioritization of resources at the operational level.

BioWatch

We found that the BioWatch program was generally consistent with the biological agents of significant concern identified in the BTRA. DHS documents state that the BTRA is to be used to update the list of threat agents monitored by BioWatch. DHS deployed BioWatch in 2003, before the release of the first BTRA in 2006.[39] Since then, DHS has reprogrammed BioWatch detection efforts once, in response to the 2006 BTRA. The BioWatch program manager told us that they review each iteration of the BTRA to ensure that the BioWatch program is aligned with the biological agents of significant concern.

We compared the lists of threat agents that have been programmed to be detected by the BioWatch program since 2006 against the biological agents of significant concern in the 2006, 2008, and 2010 BTRAs and found them generally consistent.[40]

The BioWatch program manager also told us that future generations of BioWatch are being developed to detect a larger number of biological threat agents. According to BioWatch documents, these agents are to be determined by the BTRA's risk rankings. OHA officials told us they use the BTRA to inform BioWatch because it is the most relevant CBRN risk assessment available to them and because it allows OHA to focus BioWatch detection efforts on the biological agents of significant concern.

National Bioforensic Analysis Center (NBFAC)

We found that the NBFAC used the CBRN risk assessments to partially inform its capabilities. Officials from NBFAC told us that the center used information from the BTRA to inform its priorities for developing tools needed to support their work in biological forensic attribution. Our analysis showed that the NBFAC's forensic attribution capabilities were generally consistent with the biological agents of significant concern in the BTRA.[41] However, NBFAC officials stated that because the NBFAC is mandated to maintain capabilities for other biological materials, including biological agents that are not considered high risk, future BTRA results would not necessarily lead to reprioritization of NBFAC's attribution capability development efforts.

National Biosurveillance Integration Center (NBIC)

We found that the NBIC used the CBRN risk assessments to partially inform its activities. According to the OHA branch chief responsible for the NBIC, NBIC personnel are aware of the information in DHS's CBRN risk assessments and consider this information at a strategic level. However, the NBIC could not provide us with documentation of how it had used the CBRN risk assessments to inform its capabilities at the strategic level. The NBIC branch chief also stated that NBIC does not use information from the BTRA or biological MTAs at an operational level to inform the management of their capability. The official provided documentation showing that the NBIC's mission is to collect and integrate information about biological agent detection from a variety of federal government detection systems.[42] The OHA branch chief stated that because the NBIC's mission is to integrate and provide alerts on all biological agents, including emerging and infectious diseases that are not included in the CBRN risk assessments, it is not relevant whether the biological agents the NBIC is monitoring are considered to be high risk according to the BTRA or the MTAs, although these agents are also monitored.

Select DHS Radiological and Nuclear Capabilities

Our analysis showed that DHS program managers' use of the risk assessments to inform radiological and nuclear capabilities varied from partially informing their decisions to not informing their decision at all. Officials from the NTNFC told us that because of the relatively small universe of radiological and nuclear materials, the risk rankings among these materials did not matter as much as the relative threat and consequence information for biological and chemical agents. Additionally, DHS officials told us the challenges that first responders would face in responding to a nuclear explosion in a city may be a more important concern than the type of threat material used in such an attack.

Nuclear Incident Response Teams (NIRTs)

FEMA officials told us that information from the R/NTRA appendix to the 2008 ITRA partially informed the program management of the NIRTs and FEMA's other nuclear response capabilities. Specifically, FEMA officials said that information in the R/NTRA appendix, among other sources, was used to inform FEMA's IND Response and Recovery Program.[43] Starting in 2010, FEMA officials said that NIRT-related activities were aligned with the IND Response and Recovery Program. FEMA officials told us that because of this, their management of the NIRTs is partially informed, by extension, by the R/NTRA appendix. However, FEMA could not provide us with documentation of how it specifically had used the R/NTRA appendix to inform the NIRTs.

National Technical Nuclear Forensics Center (NTNFC)

An NTNFC official told us that the NTNFC did not use information contained in the R/NTRA appendix to the 2008 ITRA, and the NTNFC does not intend to use the 2011 R/NTRA (once published) to inform its activities. The same official told us that these CBRN risk assessments do not provide useful information to inform NTNFC activities because nuclear forensic capabilities are developed for all radiological and nuclear materials, regardless of their relative risk. Further, he stated that NTNFC is already aware of the universe of possible radiological and nuclear materials that could be used to attack the nation. DHS S&T's Chief Medical and Science Advisor, the official who oversees the development of DHS's CBRN risk assessments, agreed that NTNFC's capabilities need to be able to identify all radiological and nuclear materials, and that therefore the CBRN risk assessments were not relevant for NTNFC's efforts.

SPECIFIC GUIDANCE NOT ESTABLISHED TO HELP ENSURE DHS'S CBRN RISK ASSESSMENTS ARE USED TO INFORM ITS RESPONSE PLANS AND CAPABILITIES

DHS policy states that DHS components should use risk assessment information to inform planning and capability investment decisions, but DHS has not established specific guidance, such as written procedures, that details when and how DHS components should consider using the department's CBRN-specific risk assessments to inform such activities.[44] According to the *National Strategy for Homeland Security* of 2007, the assessment and management of risk underlies all homeland security activities, including decisions about when, where, and how to invest in resources—including planning and capabilities—that eliminate, control, or mitigate risks. The TRAs and MTAs—the department's most CBRNspecific risk assessments—were used to inform to varying extents 9 of 12 response plans and 6 of 7 capabilities we analyzed, and how the risk assessments were used to inform these plans and capabilities varied. DHS officials told us that while DHS policy calls for the use of risk information to inform the department's activities, no DHS guidance specifically requires DHS officials to use the TRAs and MTAs for CBRN planning and capability investments or explains how officials should use the risk assessments to inform their decision making. As a result, the CBRN risk assessments were used to varying extents and in varying ways by DHS components for the plans and capabilities we analyzed. DHS officials said that they considered the risk assessments but chose not to use them to inform one of the plans and one of the capabilities we reviewed because they were not useful for the plan or the capability. In addition, the risk assessments were not considered at all for two of the plans we reviewed.

Since at least 2007, DHS has emphasized the need to incorporate risk information derived from risk assessments into departmental activities, and since 2009 DHS has issued a range of guidance—including an interim framework, a policy memo, a management directive, and a doctrine—on the use of such risk information. Specifically, DHS's *Interim Integrated Risk Management Framework* of January 2009 identified risk assessments as a fundamental information source for risk-informed decision making and noted that the BTRA and CTRA are examples of risk assessments produced by the department that can be used to inform risk management efforts.[45] In May 2010, the Secretary of Homeland Security issued a policy memo that requires, among other things, the use of risk assessments to inform decision making and the establishment of mechanisms for sharing risk assessments with relevant stakeholders. In March 2011, as called for in the Secretary's memo, DHS issued a management directive on integrated risk management at the department.[46] This management directive, among other things, tasks the Director of the Office of Risk Management and Analysis (RMA) within DHS's NPPD with establishing a system to facilitate the sharing of risk analysis and data across the department.[47] Further, in April 2011, DHS issued its doctrine for risk management—titled Risk Management Fundamentals—the first in a series of publications that RMA plans to issue to provide a structured approach for the distribution and employment of risk information and analysis efforts across the department.[48]

DHS's existing guidance on risk management generally identifies the importance of using risk assessments to inform departmental decision making, but it does not specifically address when and how particular risk assessments—including the TRAs and MTAs—should be considered for use by departmental entities for planning and capability investment purposes. DHS officials stated that more specific guidance has not been developed by the department or its components and agencies because they were not required to do so. However, *Standards for Internal Control in the Federal Government* state that officials should take actions, such as establishing written procedures, to help ensure that management's directives are carried out.49,50 In addition, DHS's *Interim Integrated Risk Management Framework* of January 2009 stated that DHS must establish processes that make risk information available among the department and its components and agencies when and where it is needed, noting that the ability to receive and provide meaningful and usable risk information in a timely manner requires well coordinated and established processes.

While DHS has issued guidance that generally states that risk assessments should be used to inform departmental activities, DHS could better help to ensure that its relevant CBRN-specific risk assessments— the TRAs and MTAs—are considered for use in informing CBRN-specific planning and capability investments if more specific guidance requiring such consideration is established. DHS officials also stated that establishing written procedures for such consideration could better help to ensure that officials responsible for CBRN response planning and capability investment decision making consider the CBRN risk assessments as a means to obtain current risk information for specific CBRN threat agents. This information could be used to inform the planning assumptions that CBRN response plans are designed to address, as well as the requirements development process for CBRN capabilities. In addition, DHS officials noted that the lack of written procedures requiring DHS officials to consider using the TRAs and MTAs to inform DHS's CBRN plans and capabilities could negatively affect the likelihood that future DHS officials consider using the risk assessments when planning and making investment decisions. By establishing more specific guidance that details when and how DHS components should consider using the TRAs and MTAs to inform CBRN plans and capabilities, DHS would be better positioned to ensure that officials consider and, as appropriate, incorporate the department's most detailed CBRN-specific risk information. As a result, DHS would be better positioned to ensure that its CBRN response plans and capabilities align with the assumptions and results contained within the TRAs and MTAs.

CONCLUSION

The anthrax attacks of 2001 raised concerns that the United States is vulnerable to terrorist attacks using CBRN agents. Since 2001, DHS has developed a range of CBRN risk assessments, response plans, and related capabilities to prepare for such attacks. DHS has spent at least $70 million developing these risk assessments. Using its CBRN risk assessments to help inform CBRN response planning and capability investments is consistent with DHS policy and could help to better ensure that relevant information contained in the risk assessments is used to inform such plans and capabilities. Further, given that there are thousands of CBRN agents that could potentially pose a risk to the nation in an era of declining federal budgets and constrained resources, the federal government must ensure that it is focusing its limited resources on preparing to respond to the highest risk agents. Without procedures for using the risk assessments to inform capability investment decision making, use of the assessments for such decisions may continue to vary or not occur at all. More specific guidance on when and how DHS officials should consider using the department's CBRN risk assessments to inform planning and investments could better help to ensure their consistent use and that this use is sustained beyond the tenure of any given agency official.

RECOMMENDATION FOR EXECUTIVE ACTION

To better ensure the consistent use of DHS's CBRN risk assessments at the department's components and agencies, we recommend that the Secretary of Homeland Security:

- Establish more specific guidance, including written procedures, that details when and how DHS components should consider using the department's CBRN risk assessments to inform related response plan and capability investment decision making.

AGENCY COMMENTS

We received written comments on the draft report. DHS also provided technical comments, which were incorporated as appropriate. DHS concurred with the basis for the recommendation and discussed an action that S&T—which is responsible for developing the department's CBRN risk assessments—plans to take to address the recommendation. Specifically, DHS noted that it is currently developing user guidelines for its CBRN risk assessments. In addition, DHS also stated that S&T is committed to continuing to work with relevant stakeholders to ensure that its risk assessments are useful for informing response planning and capability investment decision making.

William O. Jenkins, Jr.
Director, Homeland Security and Justice Issues

End Notes

[1] White House – Homeland Security Council, *National Strategy for Homeland Security* (Washington, D.C.: October 2007).

[2] White House, *National Security Strategy* (Washington, D.C.: May 2010).

[3] For the purposes of this report, response plans refer to strategic, conceptual, and operational CBRN scenario-specific plans and related annexes developed to define interagency roles, responsibilities, and tasks for responding to a CBRN incident. Capabilities provide the means to respond to CBRN incidents through organization, equipment, training, exercises, and personnel.

[4] GAO, *National Preparedness: DHS and HHS Can Further Strengthen Coordination for Chemical, Biological, Radiological, and Nuclear Risk Assessments*, GAO-11-606 (Washington, D.C.: June 2011).

[5] DHS also develops other non-CBRN-specific risk assessments which we did not review. TRAs assess the risks posed by CBRN agents based on variable threats, vulnerabilities, and consequences. MTAs assess the threat posed by given CBRN agents and the potential number of human exposures in plausible high-consequence scenarios. According to the *DHS Risk Lexicon*, threats are entities, actions, or occurrences, whether natural or man-made, that have or indicate the potential to harm life, information, operations, and/or property; vulnerabilities are physical features or operational attributes that render an entity, asset, system, network, or geographic area susceptible or exposed to hazards; and consequences are potential or actual effects of an event, incident, or occurrence. DHS, *DHS Risk Lexicon: 2010 Edition* (Washington, D.C.: September 2010).

[6] For the purposes of this report, we included all interagency response plans developed by DHS for responding to CBRN-specific incidents. We did not include internally developed DHS intraagency plans for CBRN events and interagency response plans that could be used to respond to CBRN incidents but that are designed for responding to all-hazards.

[7] For the purposes of this report, we define planning assumptions within the CBRN response plans as the information contained in the plans related to CBRN-specific threats, vulnerabilities, and consequences. Planning assumptions form the foundational basis upon which a response plan is developed. This understanding is necessary to enable leaders and planners to develop potential courses of action to address a given CBRN incident.

[8] GAO, *Standards for Internal Control in the Federal Government*, GAO/AIMD-00-21.3.1 (Washington, D.C.: November 1999). The criteria in GAO/AIMD 00-21.3.1, dated November 1999, issued pursuant to the requirements of the Federal Managers' Financial Integrity Act of 1982 (FMFIA), provide the overall framework for establishing and maintaining internal control in the federal government. Also pursuant to FMFIA, the Office of Management and Budget issued Circular A-123, revised December 21, 2004, to provide the specific requirements for assessing the reporting on internal controls. Internal control standards and the definition of internal control in Circular A-123 are based on GAO's *Standards for Internal Control in the Federal Government.* See also the Related GAO Products section at the end of this report.

[9] DHS, *Quadrennial Homeland Security Review* (Washington, D.C.: February 2010).

[10] DHS, *DHS Risk Lexicon: 2010 Edition* (Washington, D.C.: September 2010).

[11] DHS has standardized its risk management process to include the following steps: (1) defining and framing the context of decisions and related goals and objectives; (2) identifying the risks associated with the goals and objectives; (3) analyzing and assessing the identified risks (i.e., risk assessment); (4) developing alternative actions for managing the risks and creating opportunities, and analyzing the costs and benefits of those alternatives; (5) making a decision among alternatives and implementing that decision; and (6) monitoring the implemented decision and comparing observed and expected effects to help influence subsequent risk management alternatives and decisions. This process was codified in the DHS Interim Integrated Risk Management Framework of January 2009, and reissued in the

doctrinal document DHS Risk Management Fundamentals in April 2011. DHS, *Interim Integrated Risk Management Framework* (Washington, D.C.: January 2009) and DHS, *Risk Management Fundamentals: Homeland Security Risk Management Doctrine* (Washington, D.C.: April 2011).

[12] 42 U.S.C. § 247d-6b(c)(2)(A).

[13] For more details on DHS's TRAs and MTAs, see GAO-11-606.

[14] Since 2004, DHS determined that 14 of 17 CBRN agents that it assessed in MTAs pose a material threat to the nation and issued material threat determinations for those agents. For more details on DHS's material threat determinations, see GAO-11-606.

[15] See 42 U.S.C. § 247d-6b(c).

[16] Exec. Order No. 13,527, 75 *Fed. Reg.* 737 (Dec. 30, 2009); and White House, Homeland Security Presidential Directive 8 *(National Preparedness)* Annex I – *National Planning* (Washington, D.C.: December 2007). HSPD 8 and its Annex I were superseded by Presidential Policy Directive 8 – *National Preparedness* on March 30, 2011.

[17] DHS, *National Response Framework* (Washington, D.C.: January 2008). For the purposes of this report, we considered CBRN-specific incident annexes in the NRF to be CBRN response plans. DHS issued the National Response Plan (NRP) in December 2004 and made some revisions to the plan in May 2006 to address lessons learned from Hurricane Katrina. The National Response Framework (NRF) was issued as a full revision and replacement of the NRP in January 2008.

[18] One SGS, three STRATPLANS, and four related STRATPLAN annexes were developed under IPS for the CBRN-specific NPS prior to these planning efforts being put on an indefinite hold in July 2009 by the White House National Security Staff pending the revision of HSPD 8. Presidential Policy Directive 8 replaced HSPD 8 in March 2011.

[19] For the purposes of this report, we refer to CBRN response plans as being directly informed by DHS's CBRN risk assessments if the plans specifically identify the TRAs or MTAs as a source for information contained within the plan, or if DHS officials were able to provide documentation showing how specific information from the risk assessments was incorporated into the plan. We refer to CBRN response plans as being indirectly informed by DHS's CBRN risk assessments if DHS officials said that the TRAs or MTAs served as a source of background information that was known to officials involved in the development of the plans, but the plans do not specifically identify the risk assessments as a source for information contained in the plans and DHS officials were unable to provide documentation showing their use.

[20] DHS, *Interim National Preparedness Goal* (Washington, D.C.: March 2005) and DHS, *National Preparedness Guidelines* (Washington, D.C.: September 2007). The National Preparedness Guidelines replaced the Interim National Preparedness Goal in 2007. Both were developed to define what it means for the nation to be prepared for responding to emergencies arising from man-made or natural disasters.

[21] DHS, *National Planning Scenarios* (Washington, D.C.: April 2005). According to the National Preparedness Guidelines, the 15 National Planning Scenarios establish common assumptions regarding potential vulnerabilities and consequences posed by plausible, high-consequence natural disasters and terrorist incidents, including attacks with CBRN agents, to guide emergency response planning nationwide.

[22] White House, *Integrated Planning System* (Washington, D.C.: January 2009). The Integrated Planning System was developed to establish a standardized approach to national planning, in response to requirements in Homeland Security Presidential Directive 8 Annex I – *National Planning*.

[23] Exec. Order No. 13,527, 75 *Fed. Reg.* 737 (Dec. 30, 2009); White House, Homeland Security Presidential Directive 5 – Management of Domestic Incidents (Washington, D.C.: February 2003); and White House, Homeland Security Presidential Directive 8 – *National Preparedness,* Annex I – *National Planning* (Washington, D.C.: December 2007). In response to a requirement contained in Homeland Security Presidential Directive 5, DHS issued the National Response Plan (NRP) in December 2004 and made some revisions to the plan in May 2006 to address lessons learned from Hurricane Katrina. The National Response Framework (NRF) replaced the NRP in January 2008. HSPD 8 and its Annex I were superseded by Presidential Policy Directive 8 – *National Preparedness* on March 30, 2011.

[24] In addition to DHS, departments and agencies involved in the development of the plans under Executive Order 13527 included, among others, the Department of Health and Human Services, Department of Defense, Department of Justice, and the U.S. Postal Service.

[25] The classified anthrax MTA was published in April 2005. A for-official-use-only (FOUO) version of this MTA was published in March 2008 at the request of OHA. The FOUO version is based on the classified version of the document, but also incorporates, among other things, additional information on the health effects of such an attack as determined by officials from HHS.

[26] We omitted from this report examples from a limited set of Executive Order 13527 planning assumptions compared to CBRN risk assessment content because DHS deemed this information as sensitive or classified.

[27] These seven plans were developed and finalized for the CBRN-specific NPS prior to planning under HSPD 8 Annex I being put on indefinite hold in July 2009 by the White House National Security Staff pending the revision of HSPD 8. Presidential Policy Directive 8 – *National Preparedness* (PPD 8) superseded HSPD 8 Annex I and its provisions on March 30, 2011. For the purposes of this report, we analyzed the most detailed finalized response plans developed under HSPD 8 Annex I for a given CBRN agent. PPD 8 states that plans developed under HSPD 8 Annex I remain in effect until rescinded.

[28] HSPD 8 Annex I directed the Secretary of Homeland Security to develop strategic guidance statements (SGS), strategic plans (STRATPLANS), concept of operations plans (CONPLANS), and operational plans (OPLANS) for each NPS. SGS were to be documents that outlined strategic priorities, broad national strategic objectives, and basic assumptions; described the envisioned end state; and established the general means necessary to accomplish that end for each NPS. STRATPLANS were to be based off of the related SGS for each NPS and were to be plans that defined the mission, identified authorities, delineated roles and responsibilities, established mission-essential tasks, determined required and priority capabilities, and developed performance and effectiveness measures. CONPLANS were to be based off of the related STRATPLAN for each NPS and were to be plans that briefly described the concept of operations for integrating and synchronizing existing federal capabilities to accomplish the mission-essential tasks, and described how federal capabilities were to be integrated into and support regional, state, local, and tribal plans for each NPS. OPLANS were to be based off of the related CONPLAN for each NPS and were to be developed by each federal department and agency. These OPLANS were to be plans that identified detailed resource, personnel, and asset allocations to execute the objectives of the strategic plan and turn strategic priorities into operational execution, and were to contain the full description of the concept of operations, to include specific roles and responsibilities, tasks, integration, and actions required, with supplemental support function annexes as appropriate.

[29] IPS states that planners employ risk assessment to support, organize, and prioritize planning activities using planning scenarios and that planners should update existing plans if risk levels change based on new or updated risk assessments.

[30] For the anthrax and plague annexes to the Biological Attack STRATPLAN, DHS used FOUO versions of the anthrax and plague MTAs from 2008 that included planning assumptions from the respective classified versions of the 2005 anthrax and plague MTAs. The 2008 FOUO MTAs also incorporated consequence estimates produced by HHS officials.

[31] A chemical attack STRATPLAN was not developed prior to planning under HSPD 8 Annex I being put on indefinite hold in July 2009 by the White House National Security Staff pending HSPD 8 revision. The chemical MTAs published prior to the chemical attack SGS include MTAs that address blood agents, nerve agents, pulmonary agents, and vesicants.

[32] The foot and mouth disease annex to the Biological STRATPLAN was based on NPS #14 – *Foreign Animal Disease.*

[33] We omitted from this report examples from a limited set of HSPD 8 Annex I planning assumptions compared to CBRN risk assessment content because DHS deemed this information as sensitive or classified.

[34] The NRF includes seven incident annexes which are to address aspects of how the United States responds to particular types of incidents, two of which are specifically for CBRN threat agents.

[35] For the purposes of this report, we refer to DHS capabilities as being directly informed by DHS's CBRN risk assessments if program managers used the risk assessments to directly align the capability with the threat agents of significant concern and program managers provided us with documentation of these actions. For the purposes of this report, we refer to DHS capabilities as being partially informed by DHS's CBRN risk assessments if program managers told us they used the CBRN risk assessments, as well as other information sources, to inform the development or implementation of the capability.

[36] Department of Homeland Security, *U.S. Department of Homeland Security Strategic Plan Fiscal Years 2008-2013* (Washington, D.C.: March 2008).

[37] DHS, Integrated Risk Management (Washington, D.C.: March 2011) and DHS, *Risk Management Fundamentals: Homeland Security Risk Management Doctrine* (Washington, D.C.: April 2011).

[38] We omitted from this report a comparison of RDCDS-detectable threat agents to chemical agents of significant concern in the 2008 and 2010 CTRAs because DHS deemed this information as sensitive or classified.

[39] For more information on BioWatch and DHS's biosurveillance efforts, see GAO, *Biosurveillance: Efforts to Develop a National Biosurveillance Capability Need a National Strategy and a Designated Leader,* GAO-10-645 (Washington, D.C.: June 30, 2010).

[40] We omitted from this report a comparison of BioWatch-detectable threat agents to the biological agents of significant concern in the 2006, 2008, and 2010 BTRAs because DHS deemed this information as sensitive or classified.

[41] We omitted from this report a comparison of agents for which the NBFAC has developed attribution capabilities to the biological agents of significant concern in the 2006, 2008, and 2010 BTRAs because DHS deemed this information as sensitive or classified.

[42] The NBIC was created under the Implementing Recommendations of the 9/11 Commission Act of 2007. Pub. L. No. 110-53, § 1101, 121 Stat. 266, 375 (2007) (codified at 6 U.S.C. § 195b). NBIC is to help provide early detection and situational awareness of biological threats by integrating information and supporting the interagency biosurveillance community. For more information, see our report: *Biosurveillance: Developing a*

Collaboration Strategy Is Essential to Fostering Interagency Data and Resource Sharing, GAO-10-171 (Washington, D.C.: December 2009).

[43] This program identified IND response capability gaps at the federal, state, and local levels and reported these gaps in the *DHS Strategy for Improving the National Response and Recovery from an IND Attack* (Washington, D.C.: April 2010). FEMA is currently drafting an implementation plan for this strategy, which is intended to identify approaches to narrowing these gaps by further developing nuclear response capabilities across the nation.

[44] DHS's *Interim National Preparedness Goal* of 2005 and related *National Preparedness Guidelines* of 2007 state that DHS response plans should be informed by threat analysis and risk assessment information. Further, DHS's 2008-2013 Strategic Plan states that because the homeland security mission is complex and resources are constrained, the department will use risk assessments to inform resource decisions.

[45] DHS, *Interim Integrated Risk Management Framework* (Washington, D.C.: January 2009). This interim framework was replaced by DHS's *Risk Management Fundamentals: Homeland Security Risk Management Doctrine* in April 2011.

[46] DHS, Management Directive 007-03: *Integrated Risk Management* (Washington, D.C.: March 2011).

[47] According to RMA officials, at the completion of our review RMA was in the process of drafting instructions for implementation of Management Directive 007-03, including the operations of the DHS Risk Steering Committee. The DHS Risk Steering Committee is to serve as the governance structure to ensure collaboration and information-sharing for risk management and analysis across the department. RMA officials told us they expected to complete these instructions by late 2011.

[48] DHS, *Risk Management Fundamentals: Homeland Security Risk Management Doctrine* (Washington, D.C.: April 2011). Risk Management Fundamentals replaced DHS's Interim Risk Management Framework of 2009.

[49] GAO/AIMD-00-21.3.1.

[50] Further, internal control activities are an integral part of an entity's planning, implementing, reviewing, and accountability for stewardship of government resources and achieving effective results.

In: Risk Management …
Editor: Gustav Knudsen

ISBN: 978-1-62618-701-6

Chapter 4

PUBLISHING SCIENTIFIC PAPERS WITH POTENTIAL SECURITY RISKS: ISSUES FOR CONGRESS*

Frank Gottron and Dana A. Shea

SUMMARY

The federal government generally supports the publication of federally funded research results because wide dissemination may drive innovation, job creation, technology development, and the advance of science. However, some research results could also be used for malicious purposes. Congress, the Administration, and other stakeholders, are considering whether current policies concerning publishing such research results sufficiently balances the potential benefits with the potential harms. The current issues under debate cut across traditional policy areas, involving simultaneous consideration of security, scientific, health, export, and international policy. Because of the complexity of these issues, analysis according to one set of policy priorities may adversely affect other policy priorities. For example, maximizing security may lead to detriments in public health and scientific advancement, while maximizing scientific advancement may lead to security risks. Accounting for such trade-offs may allow policymakers to establish regulatory frameworks

* This is an edited, reformatted and augmented version of the Congressional Research Service Publication, CRS Report for Congress R42606, dated July 12, 2012.

that more effectively maximize the benefits from dual-use research while mitigating its potential risks.

The current consideration of these issues began in late 2011, when two groups of U.S. government-funded scientists submitted papers to academic journals detailing genetic modifications that increase the transmissibility of a deadly influenza strain.

Although these research results may improve pandemic influenza preparedness and response, they may also increase the probability that a highly contagious and deadly influenza strain will be introduced, either accidently or deliberately, into the human population.

Stakeholders, including the Department of Health and Human Services, the World Health Organization, journal publishers, and scientists, debated whether the possible benefits of publication outweighed the potential harms. The editors of the scientific journals decided to publish modified versions of both papers.

The controversy surrounding the publication of these influenza experiments demonstrated flaws in the existing federal mechanisms to identify and balance potential benefits of life science research and security trade-offs. Responding to these cases, the Administration released a new government-wide policy to address some of these flaws. It requires agencies that fund life science research to regularly review research portfolios and develop methods to mitigate security risks.

It is not clear whether Congress will agree with the Administration that the new policy sufficiently addresses all of the dual-use issues brought to light by this recent controversy. Congress could decide to allow the new policy to be fully implemented before evaluating whether it appropriately addresses the policy issues.

Alternatively, Congress could require agencies to implement robust processes to identify potential research of concern prior to funding; require federal prepublication review of all potential research of concern to establish appropriate limits on the distribution of the research results; require federal licensing of researchers permitted to conduct such experiments and access results; and limit such research to the most safe and secure laboratories.

This report describes the underlying controversy, the potential benefits and harms of publishing these manuscripts, the actions taken by domestic and international stakeholders, and options to improve the way research is handled to minimize security concerns.

INTRODUCTION

The federal government generally supports the publication of federally funded research results because wide dissemination may drive innovation, job creation, technology development, and the advance of science. Only in cases where security concerns rise to the level of classification does the federal government bar publication of fundamental research. This policy has led to challenges in the current era when advances in technology have lowered technical barriers in modern biological sciences making it easier for people, including potential adversaries, to reproduce biological experiments.

In late 2011, two groups of researchers receiving federal funding separately sought to publish manuscripts in scientific journals describing their successful attempts to increase the transmissibility of a highly pathogenic strain of influenza. This strain of influenza, H5N1, is sometimes referred to as avian or bird flu in the popular press. It causes severe disease in humans, but is not highly contagious between humans. Some stakeholders believe the research results should not be published. They assert that broad dissemination of such research results increases the likelihood that a highly contagious form of the virus will be introduced, either accidently or deliberately, into the human population. The federal government moved first to restrict publication of the manuscripts. Following additional discussions, the federal government recommended publishing modified versions of the manuscripts.

The debate about the publication of scientific research with potential security implications cuts across multiple policy issues, including federal support of research, maintenance of homeland security, and the flow of research information. In addition, the controversy surrounding the decision to publish these experiments demonstrated flaws in the existing mechanisms to identify and balance the potential public health benefits and security trade-offs.

Congress has acted in the past to restrict access to pathogens where the potential risk of their misuse posed a greater threat than the benefits arising from unrestricted access. Congressional policymakers may decide that research results in some areas pose similar risks and may move to impose similar limits through a variety of mechanisms. Conversely, congressional policymakers may assess the risks of information exchange to be lower and may not require additional regulation.

This report describes the underlying controversy, the potential benefits and harms of publishing these manuscripts, the actions taken by domestic and international stakeholders, and options to improve the way research is handled to minimize security concerns.

H5N1 IN NATURE

Influenza is a virus that circulates through both human and animal populations. The form of the influenza virus changes frequently, producing various strains with differing properties, including host species, levels of contagiousness, and severity of disease. Strains harmless in one host may be deadly in another. Scientists and public health officials often refer to different influenza virus strains through abbreviation. This abbreviation indicates which variety of two specific disease-related proteins (H for hemagglutinin and N for neuraminidase) the virus contains. For example, the H1N1 influenza virus caused the 2007 "swine flu" human pandemic.

A different strain, the H5N1 influenza virus, commonly known as avian or bird flu, began infecting people in China in 1997. This highly pathogenic strain had previously infected only birds. In the initial outbreak, the virus infected 18 people, 6 of whom died.[1] Since then, the virus has spread internationally, infecting humans in at least 15 countries. As of May 2012, the World Health Organization (WHO) has confirmed 604 human cases and 357 deaths from this H5N1 influenza strain.[2]

Although highly contagious among birds, the H5N1 influenza virus does not pass easily between people. Nearly all of the known human infections resulted from close contact with infected poultry. However, because viruses constantly change, future versions of H5N1 influenza virus might be more contagious among humans. If the virus did become more contagious among humans and also kept its disease-causing characteristics, a human pandemic with serious disruptions in services and social order might occur. These potential consequences drive federal investments in influenza pandemic preparedness activities, including research on various influenza strains.

H5N1 EXPERIMENTS UNDER DEBATE

While scientists know that H5N1 influenza strains naturally change over time, they do not yet understand in detail how these specific changes lead to new viral properties. Gaps in our current scientific understanding limit our ability to determine the likelihood of increased human-to-human transmission.[3] This likelihood could have important public health policy ramifications. For instance, if these changes are likely to occur, then policymakers might increase H5N1-related countermeasure development efforts. Conversely, if such changes are very unlikely or impossible, then policymakers might decrease such efforts or divert federal efforts into more pressing threats.

The National Institute for Allergy and Infectious Disease (NIAID) funded multiple researchers to determine the genetic changes that cause H5N1 strains to become more transmissible among humans. Dr. Yoshihiro Kawaoka, based at the University of Wisconsin-Madison, and Dr. Ron Fouchier, based at the Erasmus Medical Center in Rotterdam, the Netherlands, each led research groups that successfully determined such changes. Both groups used ferret-to-ferret transmission to model human-to-human transmission.[4] Independently, and using different methods, each group found specific genetic changes to the H5N1 influenza virus that make it transmissible between ferrets in separate cages.

Dr. Kawaoka's group used standard molecular biological techniques to create a ferret-transmissible H5N1 virus. The scientists took the H1N1 virus that caused the 2009 human pandemic and replaced the H1 portion with a genetically modified version of the H5 portion from an H5N1 strain. This hybrid version passed between ferrets housed in separate cages. However, this new virus, unlike the naturally occurring H5N1 virus, did not kill the ferrets. Additionally, his group found that current vaccines and antiviral medications are effective against this new hybrid strain.[5]

Dr. Fouchier's group directly infected ferrets with a genetically modified H5N1 virus. After the ferret became sick, virus from the sick ferret was used to directly infect another ferret. After multiple iterations, the H5N1 virus had changed sufficiently to become transmissible between ferrets in separate cages.[6] The scientists determined five specific genetic changes were sufficient to convey airborne transmissibility among ferrets. They found that this new strain of H5N1 was less transmissible and caused a less severe disease than naturally occurring seasonal influenza. Additionally, ferrets previously exposed to seasonal flu were immune to infection with the new H5N1 virus.[7]

The two groups submitted manuscripts to different scholarly journals. In both cases, the submission was to a publisher not based in the country where the experiments were performed. Dr. Kawaoka submitted his research conducted in the Untied States to the United Kingdom journal, *Nature*. Dr.

Fouchier submitted his research conducted in the Netherlands to the U.S. journal, *Science*.

Dual-Use Results

The manuscripts from these two groups might be described as the results of "dual-use" research. In this context, this term describes technologies or information that have the potential to both help and harm society.[8] The Department of Health and Human Services (HHS) has defined dual-use biological research as "biological research with legitimate scientific purpose that may be misused to pose a biologic threat to public health and/or national security."[9]

Balancing Potential Benefits and Harms

Policymakers and stakeholders face difficult calculations when trying to balance the potential benefits of this research against potential harms. Most public health experts agree that an influenza pandemic will occur at some indeterminate time in the future. Research on the influenza virus may provide ways to mitigate the effects of such a pandemic. However, most experts also agree that such research also increases the risk that an influenza pandemic could occur through accidental or deliberate release of a modified virus.[10] The disagreement among experts largely lies in the relative probabilities of these events. No universally accepted method exists to precisely determine these probabilities, and analysts may arrive at different, but equally valid, conclusions.

Possible Benefits

These H5N1 influenza research results provide previously unknown scientific information. In particular, this research identified some of the genes involved in transmitting the disease between mammals. Future experiments may build upon these results to further scientific understanding of how influenza virus causes disease in different animals. Such experiments could create new approaches to treating and preventing the disease.[11] Prior to this work, scientists did not know whether H5N1 virus could ever become easily transmissible between humans, and if so, how likely it would be to occur.[12] As discussed above, both groups found that some H5N1 viruses can be transmitted via airborne droplets between ferrets.

Additionally, the five mutations that Dr. Fouchier's group found sufficient to cause mammalian transmissibility have each been identified in naturally occurring H5N1 viruses.[13] This suggests the possibility that all five could appear in the same strain through natural processes. This observation has led some experts to suggest that looking for these five mutations together in nature may provide advanced warning of a coming pandemic.[14] Other experts suggest that current surveillance efforts are inadequate for this task. Additionally, focusing specifically on these mutations may cause researchers to miss other mutations that would also cause the virus to become transmissible between humans.[15] Dr. Kawaoka suggested a slightly different strategy, "rather than watching for specific mutations, it is more important to scan for the traits they bestow."[16] That type of surveillance might identify strains with human pandemic potential without relying on a list of known mutations associated with human transmission. Current surveillance efforts might require enhancement to perform such activity.

Possible Harms

Some observers believe that the H5N1 influenza research could create new threats to public health and homeland security. These threats might arise from accidental or deliberate release of H5N1 virus from a laboratory or use of the information in the published manuscripts for malicious purposes.

Possible harm from conducting these types of experiments could come from several different mechanisms. Some observers worry that modified H5N1 virus might escape from laboratories causing a human pandemic.[17] Some these experts assert that research that increases contagiousness or disease severity should not be done because of the danger posed by possible release. Although it is not possible to accurately predict how a modified virus would affect humans, some analysts warn that the 1918 influenza pandemic, which had devastating social effects, was caused by a virus with a lower fatality rate than unmodified H5N1. They assert that the potential harm from a pandemic outweighs any possible benefits from the research.[18] Other observers assert that this work can be safely conducted using appropriate precautions. For example, Dr. Fouchier and Dr. Kawaoka performed these experiments following widely accepted guidelines established by the National Institutes of Health (NIH) for working with potentially dangerous pathogens.

Other potential harms could come from adversaries. Experts highlight the possibility that published research could provide adversaries a “roadmap” to create a bioweapon.[19]

In general, scientific publication is to provide enough information so that the experiments can be replicated. Such independent verification is a cornerstone of modern science. However, experiments could be replicated for malicious purposes. It is difficult to assess the risks posed by publishing dual-use research results in general. In the present case of the H5N1 influenza manuscripts, modifying the virus independently would require additional technical knowledge and skill even with publication of experimental methods.

In addition, the transmissibility and severity of the disease the modified H5N1 virus would cause in humans is unknown. On the other hand, if the modified virus were highly transmissible between people and caused severe disease, it could cause a pandemic with devastating social effects. Given the potential effects, it is conceivable that some adversary might attempt to use these research results for malicious purposes.

STAKEHOLDER RECOMMENDATIONS

As information about the modified H5N1 influenza research results spread, various stakeholders began to debate the merits of their publication. Domestic and international groups deliberated ethical, scientific, and security issues and made recommendations.

The National Science Advisory Board for Biosecurity (NSABB) issued recommendations adopted by HHS. The World Health Organization (WHO) also issued recommendations. Science magazine, published by the American Association for the Advancement of Science (AAAS), issued statements and agreed to consider recommendations from other stakeholders.

The U.K. magazine Nature agreed to consider other stakeholder recommendations prior to publication. Many prominent international influenza scientists agreed to temporarily suspend certain influenza research to provide public policymakers time to consider issues raised by this research. The following section summarizes various stakeholder position and concerns.

National Science Advisory Board for Biosecurity (NSABB)

The NSABB is the primary federal scientific board for issues of biosecurity. It consists of experts in biological sciences, law, security, and other areas. Federal officials representing agencies that fund life sciences research serve as non-voting members. Its responsibilities include advising the Secretary of Health and Human Services and providing guidance to life scientists on dual-use research and other biosecurity issues.

Prior to the debate about the H5N1 influenza research results, the NSABB recommended a framework to help the federal government develop a comprehensive system for the "responsible identification, review, conduct, and communication of dual-use research."[20] It established certain categories of research that should draw additional attention and review. It termed this research "dual-use research of concern." The NSABB provided guidance on how to identify dual-use research of concern, recommended that individual researchers and institutions evaluate research projects for potential dual-use aspects, and identified possible ways to reduce potential harmful results of their research. However, when the H5N1 influenza research manuscripts neared publication, the federal government had yet to develop and implement a comprehensive, effective system for oversight of dual-use research of concern. As part of its advisory duties, the NSABB reviewed the submitted manuscripts and issued recommendations.

First Review

In October 2011, the NSABB initially reviewed the manuscripts. It found "that there was significant potential for harm in fully publishing these results and that the harm exceeded the benefits of publication."[21] The NSABB recommended that HHS ask the manuscript authors and the journal editors to redact certain portions of the manuscripts. Due to the importance of the findings to the public health and research communities, the NSABB recommended publishing the general conclusions but excluding the methodological and other details that could enable replication of the experiments. The NSABB also recommended adding to the manuscripts additional explanation of the goals and potential public health benefits of the research and the extensive safety and security measures taken to protect laboratory workers and the public. Also, the NSABB recommended that the U.S. government develop a mechanism for providing select access to the redacted information, stating "In order to manage the risks posed by communicating future cases of dual-use research of concern, the Board strongly urges the U.S. Government to develop in an expeditious manner a practical and secure mechanism for sharing sensitive scientific information in order to support public health, safety, and security efforts."[22] In such a manner, those scientists requiring access to the sensitive portions of the manuscripts might gain access, while the broader public and scientific community would be excluded.

Following weeks of debate among other stakeholders, including the WHO (see "World Health Organization (WHO)" below), it became apparent that the NSABB view was not uniformly shared among stakeholders. Also, practical concerns regarding the ability to establish a limited distribution network for methodological details and the ramifications of such a structure on international obligations spurred an additional review by the NSABB. The NIH requested that the manuscript authors submit revised manuscripts reflecting additional information presented during the evolving stakeholder debate to the NSABB.

Second Review

In April 2012, following a second review of the manuscripts, the NSABB reversed its earlier position, recommending the publication of both manuscripts. The members of the NSABB unanimously supported the full publication of the Kawaoka manuscript. The panel also recommended the publication of a revised version of the Fouchier manuscript on a 12-6 vote. The panel stated that it reversed its earlier recommendations on the basis of "additional information in the revised manuscripts, new non-public epidemiological information, and security information …presented in a classified briefing."[23] The majority of the panel concluded that the data would not immediately threaten public health or national security, the data may benefit public health and surveillance efforts, and the research was conducted under appropriate biosafety conditions. Factors the NSABB considered during the second review included how a decision not to fully publish would affect pandemic preparedness activities,[24] influenza research, and international relations.[25] The NSABB did not state the relative importance of these factors in reaching its decision.

One of the members that disagreed with the majority opinion on the Fouchier manuscript decision outlined his dissent in a letter to National Institutes of Health Office of Science Policy.[26] He believes that a flawed NSABB review process produced flawed decisions. The NIH wrote a letter to respond to his assertions.[27]

World Health Organization (WHO)

The World Health Organization (WHO) is the primary international forum for coordinating worldwide influenza pandemic preparedness efforts. In February 2012, after the first NSABB review but before the second, the WHO convened a small group of public health and influenza experts to discuss the publication of the H5N1 influenza manuscripts. This group of experts determined that the potential benefits of publishing the results outweighed the risks. This panel recommended publishing the results without redaction but advocated for the development of a focused communications plan. This plan would aim to increase public awareness and understanding of the significance of the H5N1 influenza studies, the rationale for their publication, and their essential biosafety and biosecurity aspects.[28]

Like the NSABB, the WHO panel discussed the concept of publishing redacted manuscripts with a mechanism for providing the restricted information to legitimate recipients. However, the WHO panel identified complications with the creation of a such a mechanism due to international agreements and national legislation.[29] One germane international agreement is the Pandemic Influenza Preparedness (PIP) Framework. This agreement links international access to influenza virus samples with sharing the benefits from research done with those samples. Some donor countries might interpret efforts to restrict access to research results as counter to the PIP Framework, possibly decreasing those countries' willingness to share virus strains.

Department of Health and Human Services (HHS)

The HHS charters and oversees the NSABB and adopted both sets of NSABB recommendations. Because the recommendations of the NSABB evolved over time, the actions and positions taken by HHS similarly evolved. Key context is the nonbinding nature of HHS actions. Even though HHS, through NIH, had funded the H5N1 influenza research, HHS actions were in response to the proposed publication of the research results by domestic and foreign publishers. The HHS has no authority over publisher activities, and a previous attempt by HHS to sway publishers regarding a manuscript with security concerns had been unsuccessful.[30]

The HHS endorsed the NSABB recommendations following the first review and issued them to both the manuscript authors and the journal editors. The HHS also stated that the U.S. government would work "to establish a mechanism to allow secure access to the information to those with a legitimate need in order to achieve important public health goals. The U.S. government is also developing a proposed oversight policy that would augment existing approaches to evaluating research that has the potential to be misused for harmful purposes."[31]

As the debate on the H5N1 influenza manuscripts progressed, HHS continued to respond to events. When scientists declared a temporary moratorium on H5N1 influenza research (see "Scientific Community" below), HHS announced that U.S. government agencies that conduct or fund such research would also abide by this moratorium.[32] Following the February 2012 WHO meeting, in which HHS representatives participated, HHS continued "to stand by the December 2011 recommendations of the National Science Advisory Board for Biosecurity (NSABB) but we intend to consider carefully the information discussed during the WHO-hosted meeting."[33]

According to NIH, the WHO-hosted meeting revealed additional information about the manuscripts. This led NIH to request that the authors submit to the NSABB revised manuscripts reflecting this information. When the NSABB recommendation changed from withholding at least part of the manuscripts to publishing the manuscripts, the HHS recommendations also changed. The HHS concurred with the new NSABB recommendation that the information in the manuscripts be communicated fully. The HHS Secretary and the NIH Director conveyed this concurrence to the journals.[34]

In addition, HHS was the vehicle for the release of new policy on dual-use life sciences research. (See "Overseeing Dual-Use Life Science Research" below.) The HHS stated that

> the recently released Federal policy on dual-use research of concern is an important step in enhancing the oversight of federally funded life sciences research going forward. Through implementation of this policy, the U.S. Government aims to preserve the benefits of vitally important life sciences research that holds the promise of enhancing quality of life for all of us, while minimizing the possibility that the knowledge, information, products, or technologies provided by such research could be misused for harm.[35]

Scholarly Publishers

As previously noted, Dr. Kawoaka and Dr. Fouchier submitted their manuscripts to the journals *Nature* and *Science* respectively. Both publishers of these journals voluntarily suspended publication of the submitted manuscripts while discussion and debate occurred. Neither journal publisher was under a mandate not to publish; the recommendations of government bodies in this case were not binding. Both journals published the manuscripts after the NSABB changed its recommendation.[36]

Since 2003, many journal editors and publishers have voluntarily adopted the responsibility of weighing the dual-use implications of submitted manuscripts.[37] These journal editors screen, review, and potentially reject manuscripts on the basis of their weapons potential. The editors developed this policy during an earlier dual-use research result publication controversy while the federal government was considering imposing new requirements through legislation or regulation.

The voluntary nature of the publisher review and the ability of a publisher to ignore non-binding government recommendations may raise questions about the efficacy of such a process. For example, the editors of *Nature* emphasized that although they voluntarily delayed publication while NSABB and WHO considered the manuscripts, they were not bound by any external recommendations. Rather, their decision to publish or not was based on internal considerations. The journal commissioned an independent risk and benefit assessment that concluded the paper should be published in full. Furthermore, the editors concluded that they will not consider redacting key details from a paper or limiting access to select recipients in the future.[38]

Relying on an editor-based effort might not sufficiently address the federal government's security concerns. Even a consensus protocol for handling dual-use research results that addresses the U.S. government's national security concerns may not stop such information from entering the open literature. The competitive, international nature of scientific publishing may lead foreign journals that lack such a protocol to legally acquire and publish material prohibited from domestic publication. Finally, with the growing ability to disseminate scientific information to a wide audience without resorting to formal publication, the effectiveness of a publisher-based policy in restricting the dissemination of contentious research is an open question.

Scientific Community

The scientific community split over the decision whether to publish the H5N1 influenza manuscripts. Some scientists supported publishing redacted versions. Others argued for full and open publication. Many prominent influenza researchers, including those that conducted the experiments in question, agreed to a voluntary, short-term moratorium on research into modified H5N1 transmission to allow some discussion of the policy issues.[39] This moratorium remains in effect.[40]

Some experts have cited this moratorium as similar to that enacted in the 1970s over genetic engineering and recombination.[41] At that time, scientists responded to criticism and public pressure by establishing a voluntary moratorium on such research. In 1975, at the Asilomar conference center in Pacific Grove, California, scientists developed a consensus statement regarding a voluntary moratorium on some types of recombinant research and an increase in security and containment requirements for other research areas. The statement and accompanying moratorium successfully allayed many, but not all, public concerns, and provided a uniform framework to address such issues. This consensus statement became the starting point for research rules developed by the National Institutes of Health Recombinant DNA Advisory Committee, which was formed to oversee such research.[42]

Issues for Congress

The controversy surrounding the decisions to publish these manuscripts highlights deficiencies in the federal decision-making processes related to dual-use life science research.[43] Congressional policymakers face many issues when considering the current debate over H5N1 influenza research. These issues include the appropriate federal government role in overseeing, funding, and publishing dual-use research activities.

Overseeing Dual-Use Life Science Research

The federal government funds a variety of life science research activities. It performs oversight of these activities through standard procedures and protocols generally identified as a contract or grant term and condition. Examples of such terms and conditions include regularly issuing technical and business reports to program managers regarding the expenditure of federal funds and complying with generally accepted best practices.

Federal agencies funding life science research do not systematically review all research-related activities, such as publication, for dual-use ramifications. To review all such activities for all federally supported life science research would place enormous burdens on the research community and the federal government. However, the current controversy highlights the flaws in the current processes to identify and mitigate potential security risks associated performing some research. Even though both H5N1 influenza researchers received federal funding, NIH, the funding agency, was unaware of the dual-use nature of the results until the manuscripts were submitted for publication.

To help correct flaws in agency process, the Administration issued new federal policy titled "United States Government Policy for Oversight of Life Sciences Dual-Use Research of Concern" on March 28, 2012.[44] This new policy aims to

> establish regular review of United States Government funded or conducted research with certain high-consequence pathogens and toxins for its potential to be dual-use research of concern (DURC) in order to: (a) mitigate risks where appropriate; and (b) collect information needed to inform the development of an updated policy, as needed, for the oversight of DURC. The fundamental aim of this oversight is to preserve the benefits of life sciences research while minimizing the risk of misuse of the knowledge, information, products, or technologies provided by such research.[45]

This new policy defines dual-use research of concern as specified types of experiments using specified pathogens or toxins that "can be reasonably anticipated to provide knowledge, information, products, or technologies that could be directly misapplied to pose a significant threat with broad potential consequences to public health and safety, agricultural crops and other plants, animals, the environment, material or national security."[46] Seven types of experiments are subject to this policy, and the pathogens and toxins covered by this policy are also regulated as select agents.[47]

This new policy requires every federal department and agency to review all sponsored life science research projects and identify those that meet the dual-use research of concern criteria. The sponsoring agency must "assess the risks and benefits of such projects, including how research methodologies may generate risks and/or whether open access to the knowledge, information, products, or technologies generates risk."[48] This policy directed departments and agencies to report the results of their reviews to the Assistant to the President for Homeland Security and Counterterrorism within 90 days. In the future, such reviews and reports are to occur biannually.

Based on this assessment, and in collaboration with the institution or researcher, the agency must develop a risk mitigation plan. When appropriate, the agency is to incorporate the risk mitigation plan into the grant, contract, or work agreement with the researcher. For existing projects, the agency should consider modifying the existing agreement or seek voluntary implementation of the risk mitigation plan. For proposed projects that have not yet been funded, the agency is to consider incorporating a risk mitigation plan into the grant, contract, or agreement. The policy does not require specific risk mitigation procedures, but contains examples, such as modifying the design or conduct of the research; performing periodic progress reviews by the agency; and determining how the results will be published or otherwise communicated. If the agency determines that risk mitigation efforts prove insufficient, the agency is to consider requesting voluntary redaction of any publication or communication; classifying the research; or terminating project funding.

In accordance with the new policy, NIH conducted its review and found 381 extramural and 404 intramural projects using pathogens or toxins covered by the new policy. Of these projects, NIH designated 10 extramural and no intramural projects as dual-use research of concern. Seven of the designated dual-use research of concern projects use influenza virus, while one project each uses the pathogens that cause anthrax, plague, and botulism.[49] The NIH is determining which risk mitigation steps are appropriate for each case.[50]

Once fully implemented, this policy might address some of the deficiencies highlighted by the recent publishing controversy. Reviews of proposed research and periodic reviews of funded research might alert the funding agency of potentially challenging results early enough for agencies to mitigate their potential harmful effects. However, some of the risk mitigation steps in this policy including the use of prepublication manuscript review and the possibility of limiting distribution of research results raise additional issues that likely complicate implementation of this policy.

Publishing Dual-Use Research Results

The federal government generally supports the open publication of unclassified, federally funded research results. Many federal grants and contracts supporting scientific research urge the publication of research results. The current federal policy, as described in National Security Decision Directive 189, is that access to fundamental research results should remain unrestricted, and that in the rare case where it is necessary to restrict such information, classification is the appropriate mechanism.[51] For non-fundamental research, additional mechanisms may be used to restrict dissemination, such as contract clauses related to release of information and export controls. Implementation of the new dual-use research of concern policy may create significant exceptions to this general policy.[52]

Prepublication Review and Export Control

The Department of Commerce regulates the export of some dual-use technologies and research results.[53] It administers the Export Administration Regulations (EAR), which apply to technologies (and technical information) listed on the Commerce Control List (CCL). The CCL includes the pathogens and toxins covered by the new federal dual-use research of concern policy. Noncompliance with export controls can result in fines and imprisonment.

Research that qualifies as "fundamental research" is exempt from export controls.[54] To qualify as "fundamental research," research activities must be ordinarily published and shared broadly within the scientific community. They must also be free of prepublication review, except for purposes of determining whether proprietary information is being divulged or patent rights are being compromised. Thus, information resulting from government-sponsored research where the government has required prepublication review for national security reasons is not "fundamental research." Research funded with such prepublication agreements would be subject to export regulation and potential control.

The concept of "deemed export" further complicates this issue. A deemed export is transfer of information, not physical items, to a foreign national within the United States.[55]

Research conducted under a grant or contract that contained prepublication review provisions would not qualify as fundamental research and thus might increase the likelihood that a deemed export violation might occur.

Without the protection of the fundamental research exemption foreign students and researchers conducting research or attending graduate-level classes may be exposed to information relating to technology which falls under export controls. Such information transfer may require an export license and may be completely prohibited for some foreign nationals. In contrast, equivalent research conducted under a grant or contract without prepublication review provisions would likely qualify as "fundamental research," would not require an export license, and would not raise deemed export issues.

Limited Access to Research Results

In order to address the security challenges presented by the H5N1 influenza manuscripts, the NSABB recommended that the government develop a mechanism to provide controlled access to sensitive scientific information:

> …the Board also recognizes that research findings will likely emerge in the very near future that should not be widely disseminated because of a high risk of misuse but that nevertheless should be made available to certain researchers and public health officials around the world who have a legitimate need to know. The need for an effective, practical, and feasible mechanism for selectively sharing sensitive scientific information has never been more apparent. In order to manage the risks posed by communicating future cases of dual-use research of concern, the Board strongly urges the U.S. Government to develop in an expeditious manner a practical and secure mechanism for sharing sensitive scientific information in order to support public health, safety, and security efforts.[56]

The HHS initially endorsed this approach and began exploring how to establish such a mechanism.

Limiting general access to nonproprietary research results has several challenges, both practical and philosophical in nature. These challenges include the need to identify what entity would establish the infrastructure to store and retain control of the restricted information; how access to the restricted information can be assessed for current and future researchers; what penalties or other mechanism would be invoked to limit secondary dissemination of the information, either through subsequent publication of research building on the restricted information or through more informal information exchange; and how to facilitate restricted information exchange across international borders in order to meet treaty and other obligations.

Experts have questioned the effectiveness of such controls.[57] Scientists and other professionals regularly exchange preliminary information through seminars, conferences, and other informal gatherings. If, at a later date, federal government deems such information should be restricted, it may be difficult or impossible for the government to prevent its spread. Similarly, publishers of scientific research generally distribute information, not restrict information, and may lack the infrastructure or inclination to compartmentalize information with respect to their subscribers. For example, the editors of *Nature* have stated that they will not consider limiting distribution of any data that has been submitted to them.[58] The editors of *Science* support the development of an international system to provide access to information deemed not freely publishable to those with a "need to know."[59]

International ramifications of a limited access approach may be significant. The WHO determined that controlling the distribution of influenza research results would likely damage worldwide pandemic influenza preparedness by reducing the willingness of countries to share samples of influenza virus. In addition, other countries export regulations might limit dissemination of such restricted information, requiring further harmonization with treaty obligations and mechanisms to determine scientific credentials.[60]

These challenges may be surmountable with sufficient federal investment. The federal government maintains information with access restrictions, has several databases of publications and/or best practices, and oversees a credentialing system for researchers who wish physical access to certain pathogens known as select agents. While these systems do not currently serve the purpose of limiting access to dual-use research results, they may provide a potential model for developing necessary systems.

Funding Dual-Use Research

A key component of the new policy on dual-use life sciences research is the identification of the dual-use nature of research programs when they begin. The federal government historically has funded a wide array of research including that with dual-use implications. The prevailing rationale for supporting such research is the belief that the benefits from dual-use research outweigh the potential risks of misuse since many more people will use it for beneficial purposes than for malicious ends.

The new policy requires each funding agency to review its research portfolio and identify those research activities that are potential dual-use research of concern. Review of research activities at the funding stage raises several policy challenges, including the completeness of such a review, the mechanism for identifying research projects, and the mechanism for assessing risk and its mitigation. While this policy initially may identify some dual-use research of concern, it also may not identify all dual-use research of concern. In some cases, the research results that might qualify as dual-use research of concern arise unexpectedly out of the research activities. Periodic review of on-going research projects could identify these unforeseen results, but may create its own set of challenges.

The effort to review existing research activities may require clear guidance and oversight. Federal agencies often fund dual-use research, only some of which is potentially of concern. Of that smaller number of research activities, an even smaller number are actually of concern. Thus, those program managers or other officials reviewing research projects could spend most of their reviews identifying activities that are not dual-use research of concern. This may affect the accuracy of review if program managers develop expectations regarding their research portfolio based on past reviews.

In addition, some experts have argued that the dual-use implications of a research activity vary depending on an analyst's perspective. Some analysts, for example, question whether the risks of federal biodefense research activities outweigh the potential benefits.[61] The experience and expertise of officials or scientists performing the risk and benefit assessment may vary between or within agencies, which could lead to inconsistent appreciation of risks or benefits.

Scope

Concomitant with the other policy considerations is the issue of how broadly to apply new federal dual-use policies. The new dual-use research of concern policy discussed above is limited to government-sponsored life science research using a few specific organisms and toxins for defined types of experiments. This policy does not encompass other research or technologies outside this scope which may pose equivalent risk and benefit trade-offs.

Once fully implemented, this policy may not identify all government-sponsored life science research with potentially significant national security concerns. The list of covered organisms and toxins does not include all those that have been deemed by the federal government to pose a significant potential threat to national security or public health in other contexts, such as under the select agent regulations[62] or included as NIAID Category A, B, and C priority pathogens. Thus, research on such pathogens that increases their harmful effects or decreases their response to countermeasures would not be identified by this policy.

Additionally, research on unlisted pathogens that could also apply to related covered pathogens may not be identified by this policy. In 2001, researchers serendipitously discovered modifications to mousepox virus that rendered mousepox vaccination in mice ineffective. This raised fears that similar modification to the closely related smallpox virus would render smallpox vaccination in humans ineffective.[63] It is not clear that the new dual-use research of concern policy would identify this type of research.

Another challenge may come from emerging technologies. Non-life science research may produce enabling technologies that increase the risk of malicious use of the pathogens and toxins covered by the dual-use research of concern policy. For example, advances in encapsulation or aerosolization technologies could significantly increase the effectiveness of the malicious use of one of the listed pathogens. Such research, although possibly directly applicable to increasing the risk of bioterrorism, appears unlikely to be identified by this new dual-use research of concern policy.

Stakeholders may also note that this new policy applies only to government sponsored research. However, the government only funds about 53% of basic research and 42% of applied research conducted domestically.[64] Research not sponsored by the government is not covered by this new dual-use research of concern policy. Broadening the scope of the new policy on federal oversight of dual-use research of concern may address many of these potential shortcomings. However, such broadening will likely increase the administrative burden on both the research community and government agencies. Additionally, extending oversight to include non-government-sponsored research will likely raise additional issues such as appropriate enforcement mechanisms and possible decrease in international competitiveness.

OPTIONS FOR CONGRESS

Congressional policymakers have a variety of options before them. They may decide that the current policy framework serves as a good starting point and allow the executive branch to further develop and implement the proposed policies. Alternatively congressional policymakers might increase oversight activities and direct the Administration, either through hearings, report language, or legislation, to take specific actions to address scientific or security concerns.

Allow Current Policy Framework to Develop

Policymakers may choose to continue to allow the executive branch to address dual-use research concerns through the NSABB, voluntary advisory processes with publishers, and the new government-wide dual-use research of concern policy. Federal agencies are currently developing policies and procedures to implement the new dual-use research of concern policy. Congress could decide to wait to act until agencies complete implementation before determining whether the new policies adequately address the deficiencies highlighted by the recent H5N1 influenza manuscripts. Alternatively, Congress could decide to more closely monitor the development and implementation of these policies through oversight activities such as requests for information from the Administration or additional oversight hearings.[65]

Change Current Policy Framework

Rather than rely solely on executive branch action, congressional policymakers might choose to increase oversight activities or introduce legislation to provide greater direction or focus to the Administration, or to directly address perceived policy gaps. Alternatively, Congress could agree with the overall policy direction but decide that codifying the policies in statute would more effectively address the issues.

Early Identification of Dual-Use Research of Concern

Congressional policymakers interested in the extent of dual-use research funded by the federal government might direct funding agencies to identify and tabulate prospective dual-use concerns prior to funding the research. Since the federal government lacks a fully implemented framework to assess or value such dual-use research concerns currently, congressional policymakers likely would need to formalize the criteria against which such research would be measured. Measures developed by the NSABB and the dual-use research of concern policy might apply. Assessment of all research activities might require significant investment by executive branch agencies, due to the large number of research grants and contracts awarded by the federal government annually. Such concerns might be weighed against the prospective benefits to assess the dual-use impact of the research investment and risk mitigation measures used to manage the risk and benefit relationship.

Voluntary or mandatory prepublication review for federally funded research or the development of new funding opportunities containing prepublication review as a condition of acceptance may improve the government's ability to identify and mitigate dual-use concerns of particular results. Individual funding vehicles have been offered to universities which would provide the funding agency with access to research results prior to publication.[66]

Opponents of this approach cite the general unwillingness that universities have towards restricted research funding.[67] Some universities have explicit policies barring acceptance of federal funding requiring prepublication review. Also, scientists may not be as willing to work in research areas where publication is not allowed as in areas where publication is encouraged.[68] As a consequence, the pool of eligible scientists competing for federal funding might decrease, potentially lowering the quality of research and development performed in these areas. Additionally, determining at the funding stage whether research will lead to sensitive results is considered difficult. For example, the previously cited mousepox experiments were part of a fertility research program aimed at techniques for pest control, and the results of the experiment were unexpected.[69]

Alternatively, congressional policymakers might identify the recipients of research funding as more appropriate to perform the review. In such an approach, federal agencies might require contract and grant recipients to identify when their research activities either have, or might be expected to produce, dual-use ramifications. Again, the criteria against which recipients would judge their research activities would have to be identified. As with the federal review option, a framework and guidance would need to be established.[70]

Prepublication Review of Dual-Use Results

Congressional policymakers might increase federal oversight by mandating federal funding agencies perform prepublication review of dual-use research results and identify those publications with security concerns. The NSABB recommended the government develop mechanisms for limiting distribution.[71] If combined with credentialing scientists able to receive such information, potentially in a manner similar to select agent registration, this approach could allow scientists with appropriate credentials or need-to-know access to such scientific literature, but would bar others' access. Access to such information might be controlled by the federal government or by the publisher through secure, password-controlled websites.[72] Other options might include dissemination of such material via professional societies.

Opponents of such an approach cite the logistical difficulties in determining those scientists with a *bona fide* reason for access to this information; determining how and in what manner application the dual-use label would be implemented; and determining how such material would be disseminated to those scientists eligible to receive it. Additionally, some scientists or universities might choose not to participate in a process which would determine access eligibility, especially if the process lacked transparency or was viewed as potentially arbitrary.[73]

Another concern is the effectiveness of such a federally based review. The federal government funds about 31% of the total research and development efforts in the United States. In terms of basic and applied research, the federal government funds 53% and 42% respectively.[74] If prepublication review resides within the federal government, in contrast to a voluntary submission to professional societies or an ethical or moral statement developed and overseen by journal publishers, then all basic and applied research would not be reviewed.

Many members of the scientific community strongly believe that all unclassified scientific results including all information necessary to reproduce an experiment should be shared widely.[75] Some observers believe that efforts to restrict access to the data will be impractical or ineffective.[76] However, in contrast, some prominent members of the scientific community support developing such a system.[77]

Finally, some universities may fear that federal prepublication review to determine whether the results pose a security risk would invalidate the fundamental research exemption that such research results normally enjoy. As a consequence, university research done in an export-controlled area might not be excluded from export control regulations (see "Prepublication Review and Export Control").

Federal Licensing of Research

Congressional policymakers might believe that the role of the federal government should be expanded beyond a gatekeeping role when considering dual-use biological research. Since much research that has potential terrorism concerns also may play a role in biodefense, it has been suggested that such research should continue, but only performed by select researchers at specific facilities. For example, a national federal authority might license qualified researchers and research facilities and oversee research by licensed researchers in licensed facilities.[78] Some scientists have asserted that licensing researchers, facilities, or experiments would have a strong, negative impact on scientific productivity in those areas.[79] However, the registration of life scientists wishing to work with select agents has shown though that some scientists are willing to engage in such licensed research.[80] Such a licensing approach might limit the rate of advance of scientific discovery due to the lessened amount of discussion and degree of research diversity. Additionally, in influenza research this approach may be incompatible with international agreements and increase the difficulty of obtaining viral samples from endemic countries.

Increase Biosafety Level

Congressional policymakers could reduce the risk of accidental release of modified H5N1 influenza strains by requiring such research to be done at a higher biosafety level (BSL). Some experts assert requiring such research to be conducted only at the highest level of biosafety containment and under the most secure conditions would effectively reduce the possibility of an accidental release or a deliberate release by a disgruntled or disturbed laboratory worker.[81] Current requirements for H5N1 influenza research require research activities to be done at the BSL 3 level. Many laboratories meet the BSL 3 standards. In contrast, the number of BSL 4 laboratories, built to a much more stringent—and expensive—standard, is significantly smaller, even though the number of BSL 4 laboratories has increased since 2001. Increasing the required biosafety level would limit the number of locations where the research could be performed and the number of researchers with access. Canada has increased the required biosafety level from BSL 3 to BSL 4 following a review of the various risks.[82]

While increasing the biosafety level might limit the risks of an unintentional release due to biocontainment failure, it would also likely limit the rate of scientific advance. Such limitations could arise, for example, from logistical issues, such as insufficient research space for the number of interested researchers; and cost issues, due to the higher overhead cost for performing work in a BSL 4 laboratory. As a consequence, congressional policymakers may wish to balance both the potential outcomes and the potential likelihood of events. For example, increasing near-term biosafety may make it less likely that a release of transmissible H5N1 virus occurs due to a laboratory accident, but at the potential cost of not having important research results to mitigate potentially more likely naturally occurring outbreak of transmissible H5N1 influenza.

CONCLUSION

Policymakers faced with assessing dual-use issues are particularly challenged by the multidisciplinary nature of dual-use activities. Dual-use issues cut across traditional policy areas, involving simultaneous consideration of security, scientific, health, export, and international policy. Because of the complexity of dual-use issues, analysis of a topic according to one set of policy priorities may lead to unforeseen complications due to its intersection with other policy priorities. For example, maximizing security may lead to detriments in public health and scientific advancement, while maximizing scientific advancement may lead to security risks. Accounting for such trade-offs may allow policymakers to establish regulatory frameworks that more effectively maximize the benefits from dual-use research while mitigating its potential risks.

End Notes

[1] World Health Organization, *H5N1 Avian Influenza: Timeline of Major Events*, April 20, 2012; http://www.who.int/influenza/human_animal_interface/H5N1_avian_influenza_update200412.pdf.

[2] World Health Organization, *Cumulative Number of Confirmed Human Cases for Avian Influenza A (H5N1) Reported to WHO, 2003-2012*, May 29, 2012. For the most current data available, see http://www.who.int/influenza/human_animal_interface/H5N1_cumulative_table_archives/en/index.html.

[3] Li-Mei Chen, Ola Blixt, and James Stevens, et al., "In Vitro Evolution of H5N1 Avian Influenza Virus Toward Human-Type Receptor Specificity," *Virology*, vol. 422 (November 5, 2011), pp. 105-113; and Martin Enserink, "Controversial Studies Give Deadly Flu Virus Wings," *Science*, vol. 334 (December 2, 2011), p. 1192.

[4] Most scientists agree that ferrets are an appropriate animal model for such studies; however, the new viruses may act differently in humans. They may have different transmissibility or disease severity in humans than they do in ferrets. See Anthony S. Fauci and Francis S. Collins, "Benefits and Risks of Influenza Research: Lessons Learned," *Science*, vol. 336 (June 22, 2012), pp. 1522-1523.

[5] Yoshihiro Kawaoka, "Flu Transmission Work Is Urgent," *Nature*, published online January 25, 2012, http://www.nature.com/nature/journal/vaop/ncurrent/full/nature10884.html; and Masaki Imai, Tokiko Watanabe, Masato Hatta, et al., "Experimental Adaptation of an Influenza H5 HA Confers Respiratory Droplet Transmission to a Reassortant H5 HA/H1N1 Virus in Ferrets," *Nature*, published online, May 2, 2012, http://www.nature.com/nature/journal/vaop/ncurrent/full/nature10831.html.

[6] Sander Herfst, Eefje J.A. Schrauwen, and Martin Linster, et al., "Airborne Transmission of Influenza A/H5N1 Virus Between Ferrets," *Science*, vol. 336 (June 22, 2012), pp. 1534-1541.

[7] Ron Fouchier, "H5N1 Research Discussion," Panel discussion at the American Society for Microbiology Biodefense and Emerging Infectious Disease Research Meeting, Washington, DC, February 29, 2012, http://www.asmbiodefense.org/index.php/program-information/nsabbs-recommendations-for-h5n1-research; and Sander Herfst, Eefje J.A. Schrauwen, and Martin Linster, et al., "Airborne Transmission of Influenza A/H5N1 VirusBetween Ferrets," *Science*, vol. 336 (June 22, 2012), pp. 1534-1541.

[8] Historically, the term "dual-use" has referred to technologies that have both a military and a civilian application.

[9] Department of Health and Human Services, National Science Advisory Board for Biosecurity Charter, March 4, 2004.

[10] Declan Butler, "Fears Grow over Lab-bred Flu," *Nature*, vol. 480 (December 22, 2011), pp. 421–422; and Marc Lipsitch, Joshua B. Plotkin, and Lone Simonsen, et al., "Evolution, Safety, and Highly Pathogenic Influenza Viruses," *Science*, vol. 336 (June 22, 2012), pp. 1529-1531.

[11] Ron A.M. Fouchier, Sander Herfst, and Albert D.M.E. Osterhaus, "Restricted Data on Influenza H5N1 Virus Transmission," *Science*, vol. 335 (February 10, 2012), pp. 662-663; and Masaki Imai, Tokiko Watanabe, Masato Hatta, et al., "Experimental Adaptation of an Influenza H5 HA Confers Respiratory Droplet Transmission to a Reassortant H5 HA/H1N1 Virus in Ferrets," *Nature*, published online, May 2, 2012, http://www.nature.com/nature/journal/vaop/ncurrent/full/nature10831.html.

[12] National Science Advisory Board for Biosecurity, "Policy: Adaptations of Avian Flu Virus Are a Cause for Concern," *Nature*, vol. 482 (January 31, 2012), pp. 153–154.

[13] Declan Butler, "Caution Urged for Mutant Flu Work," *Nature*, vol. 481 (January 25, 2012), pp.421-422; and Sander Herfst, Eefje J.A. Schrauwen, and Martin Linster, et al., "Airborne Transmission of Influenza A/H5N1 Virus Between Ferrets," *Science*, vol. 336 (June 22, 2012), pp. 1534-1541.

[14] Declan Butler, "Caution Urged for Mutant Flu Work," *Nature*, vol. 481 (January 25, 2012), pp.421-422.

[15] Paul S. Keim, "Q&A: Reasons for Proposed Redaction of Flu Paper," *Nature*, published online, January 31, 2012, http://www.nature.com/nature/journal/vaop/ncurrent/full/482156a.html.

[16] Ed Yong, "Mutant-flu Paper Published," *Nature*, vol. 485 (May 3, 2012), pp. 13-14.

[17] Thomas Inglesby, "Engineered H5N1: A Rare Time for Restraint in Science," *Annals of Internal Medicine*, vol. 156 (March 20, 2012), pp. 460-462; Lynn Klotz and Ed Sylvester, "Worry About Lab Infections," *Nature*, vol. 481 (January 15, 2012), pp. 257-259; and Marc Lipsitch, Joshua B. Plotkin, and Lone Simonsen, et al., "Evolution, Safety, and Highly Pathogenic Influenza Viruses," *Science*, vol. 336 (June 22, 2012), pp. 1529-1531.

[18] Thomas Inglesby, "Engineered H5N1: A Rare Time for Restraint in Science," *Annals of Internal Medicine*, vol. 156 (March 20, 2012), pp. 460-462; Lynn Klotz and Ed Sylvester, "Worry About Lab Infections," *Nature*, vol. 481 (January 15, 2012), pp. 257-259.

[19] National Science Advisory Board for Biosecurity, "Policy: Adaptations of Avian Flu Virus Are a Cause for Concern," *Nature*, vol. 482 (January 31, 2012), pp. 153–154.

[20] National Science Advisory Board for Biosecurity, "Proposed Framework for the Oversight of Dual-Use Life Sciences Research: Strategies for Minimizing the Potential Misuse of Research Information," June 2007.

[21] National Science Advisory Board for Biosecurity, "Policy: Adaptations of Avian Flu Virus Are a Cause for Concern," *Nature*, vol. 482 (January 31, 2012), pp. 153–154.

[22] National Science Advisory Board for Biosecurity, *Findings and Recommendations,* March 29-30, 2012, p. 6, http://www.nih.gov/about/director/03302012_NSABB_Recommendations.pdf.

[23] National Science Advisory Board for Biosecurity, *Findings and Recommendations,* March 29-30, 2012, p. 2, http://www.nih.gov/about/director/03302012_NSABB_Recommendations.pdf

[24] Robert Webster, "Case Study: H5N1 Avian Influenza," Presentation at National Academies of Science workshop "Issues Raised, Lessons Learned, and Paths Forward for Dual-Use Research in the Life Sciences: The H5N1Controversy", Washington, DC, May 1, 2012, http://sites.nationalacademies.org/PGA/stl/H5N1/index.htm.

[25] Testimony of Paul S. Keim, Ph.D., Acting Chairman, National Science Advisory Board for Biosecurity, National Institutes of Health, U.S. Department of Health and Human Services, before the Senate Committee on Homeland Security and Governmental Affairs, April 26, 2012.

[26] Letter from Michael T. Osterholm, Director of the Center for Infectious Disease Research and Policy, to Amy P.Patterson, Associate Director for Science Policy, National Institutes of Health, April 12, 2012, http://news.sciencemag.org/scienceinsider/NSABB%20letter %20final%2041212_3.pdf.

[27] Letter from Amy P. Patterson, Associate Director for Science Policy, National Institutes of Health, to Michael T. Osterholm, Director of the Center for Infectious Disease Research and Policy, April 25, 2012, http://blogs.nature.com/news/files/2012/05/Response-to-Dr-Osterholm-04-25-2012.pdf.

[28] World Health Organization, *Report on Technical Consultation on H5N1 Research Issues*, February 16, 2012, p.3, http://www.who.int/influenza/human_animal_interface/ mtg_report_h5n1.pdf.

[29] World Health Organization, *Report on Technical Consultation on H5N1 Research Issues*, February 16, 2012, p.4, http://www.who.int/influenza/human_animal_interface/ mtg_report_h5n1.pdf.

[30] Jocelyn Kaiser, "PNAS Publishes Botulinum Paper," *Science*, vol. 309, July 1, 2005, p. 31.

[31] National Institutes of Health, Department of Health and Human Services, *Press Statement on the NSABB Review of H5N1 Research*, December 20, 2011.

[32] Francis S. Collins, Director, National Institutes of Health, Department of Health and Human Services, and Anthony S. Fauci, Director, National Institute of Allergy and Infectious Diseases, Department of Health and Human Services, *NIH Statement on H5N1*, January 20, 2012.

[33] Francis S. Collins, Director, National Institutes of Health, Department of Health and Human Services, *NIH Statement on H5N1 and the World Health Organization Meeting*, February 17, 2012.

[34] Francis S. Collins, Director, National Institutes of Health, Department of Health and Human Services, *Statement by NIH Director Francis Collins, M.D., Ph.D. on the NSABB Review of Revised H5N1 Manuscripts*, April 20, 2012.

[35] Francis S. Collins, Director, National Institutes of Health, Department of Health and Human Services, *Statement by NIH Director Francis Collins, M.D., Ph.D. on the NSABB Review of Revised H5N1 Manuscripts*, April 20, 2012.

[36] Masaki Imai, Tokiko Watanabe, Masato Hatta, et al., "Experimental Adaptation of an Influenza H5 HA Confers Respiratory Droplet Transmission to a Reassortant H5 HA/H1N1 Virus in Ferrets," *Nature*, published online, May 2, 2012; and Sander Herfst, Eefje J.A. Schrauwen, and Martin Linster, et al., "Airborne Transmission of InfluenzaA/H5N1 Virus Between Ferrets," *Science*, vol. 336 (June 22, 2012), pp. 1534-1541.

[37] Journal Editors and Authors Group, "Uncensored Exchange of Scientific Results," *Proceedings of the National Academy of Science*, vol. 100, February 18, 2003, p. 1464.

[38] Editorial, "Publishing Risky Research," *Nature*, published online, May 2, 2012.

[39] Ron A. M. Fouchier, Adolfo García-Sastre, and Yoshihiro Kawaoka, et al., "Pause on Avian Flu Transmission Studies," *Nature*, vol. 481 (January 26, 2012), p. 443; and World Health Organization, *Report on Technical Consultation on H5N1 Research Issues*, February 16, 2012, p.4, http://www.who.int/influenza/human_animal_interface/mtg_report_h5n1.pdf.

[40] David Malakoff, "How Much Longer Will the Moratorium Last?" *Science*, vol. 336 (June 22, 2012), pp. 1495-1496.

[41] Paul S. Keim, "Q&A: Reasons for Proposed Redaction of Flu Paper," *Nature*, published online January 31, 2012, http://www.nature.com/nature/journal/vaop/ncurrent/full/482156a.html.

[42] An overview of the Asilomar conference can be read in Donald S. Fredrickson's "Asilomar and Recombinant DNA: The End of the Beginning," found in *Biomedical Politics*, (Washington, DC: National Academy Press), 1991, pp. 258-298.

[43] For a historical perspective on the development of current policy framework, see Gerald L. Epstein, "Preventing Biological Weapon Development Through the Governance of Life Science Research," *Biosecurity and Bioterrorism: Biodfense Strategy, Practice, and Science*, vol. 10, no. 1 (2012).

[44] *United States Government Policy for Oversight of Life Sciences Dual-Use Research of Concern*, March 28, 2012. http://oba.od.nih.gov/oba/biosecurity/pdf/united_states_ government_policy_for_oversight_of_durc_final_version_032812.pdf.

[45] *United States Government Policy for Oversight of Life Sciences Dual-Use Research of Concern*, March 28, 2012. http://oba.od.nih.gov/oba/biosecurity/pdf/united_states_ government_policy_for_oversight_of_durc_final_version_032812.pdf.

[46] *United States Government Policy for Oversight of Life Sciences Dual-Use Research of Concern*, March 28, 2012. http://oba.od.nih.gov/oba/biosecurity/pdf/ united_ states_government_policy_for_oversight_of_durc_final_version_032812.pdf

[47] The possession, use, and transfer of all of the pathogens and toxins covered by this policy are also subject to the select agent regulations (see 7 C.F.R. 331, 9 C.F.R. 121, 42 C.F.R. 72, and 42 C.F.R. 73).

[48] *United States Government Policy for Oversight of Life Sciences Dual-Use Research of Concern*, March 28, 2012. http://oba.od.nih.gov/oba/biosecurity/pdf/ united_states_government_policy_for_oversight_of_durc_final_version_032812.pdf

[49] Testimony of Anthony S. Fauci, M.D., Director, National Institute of Allergy and Infectious Diseases, National Institutes of Health, U.S. Department of Health and Human Services, before the Senate Committee on Homeland Security and Governmental Affairs, April 26, 2012.

[50] Testimony of Anthony S. Fauci, M.D., Director, National Institute of Allergy and Infectious Diseases, National Institutes of Health, U.S. Department of Health and Human Services, before the Senate Committee on Homeland Security and Governmental Affairs, April 26, 2012.

[51] White House, Executive Office of the President, "National Policy on the Transfer of Scientific, Technical and Engineering Information," *National Security Decision Directive-189*, 1985.

[52] Mark S. Frankel, "Regualting the Boundries of Dual-Use Research," *Science*, vol. 336 (June 22, 2012), pp. 1523-1525.

[53] For more on export controls, see CRS Report R41916, *The U.S. Export Control System and the President's Reform Initiative*, by Ian F. Fergusson and Paul K. Kerr.

[54] 15 C.F.R. 734.3(b)(3)(ii).

[55] For more on deemed export issues, see the Department of Commerce Bureau of Industry and Security's Deemed Export FAQ at http://www.bis.doc.gov/deemedexports/ deemedexports faqs.html.

[56] National Science Advisory Board for Biosecurity, *Findings and Recommendations,* March 29-30, 2012, p. 6, http://www.nih.gov/about/director/03302012_NSABB_Recommendations. pdf.

[57] Bruce Schneier, "Securing Medical Research: A Cybersecurity Point of View," *Science*, vol. 336 (June 22, 2012), pp. 1527-1529.

[58] Editorial, "Publishing Risky Research," *Nature*, published online, May 2, 2012.

[59] Bruce Alberts, "H5N1," *Science*, vol. 336 (June 22, 2012), p. 1524.

[60] Ron A.M. Fouchier, Sander Herfst, and Albert D.M.E. Osterhaus, "Restricted Data on Influenza H5N1 Virus Transmission," *Science*, vol. 335 (February 10, 2012), pp. 662-663.

[61] Malcolm Dando, *The United States National Institute of Allergy and Infectious Diseases (NIAID) Research Programme on Biodefense: A Summary and Review of Varying Assessments*, Bradford Disarmament Research Center (Bradford, UK), July 2004.

[62] 42 C.F.R. 73, 7 C.F.R. 331, and 9 C.F.R. 121.

[63] Ronald J. Jackson, Alistair J. Ramsay, Carina D. Christensen, et al., "Expression of Mouse Interleukin-4 by a Recombinant Ectromelia Virus Suppresses Cytolytic Lymphocyte Responses and Overcomes Genetic Resistance to Mousepox," *Journal of Virology*, vol. 75, February 2001, pp. 1205-1210.

[64] Percentages presented for 2009. Mark Boroush, National Science Foundation, *U.S. R&D Spending Suffered a Rare Decline in 2009 but Outpaced the Overall Economy*, NSF 12-310, March 2012.

[65] For examples, see Letter from Congressman F. James Sensenbrenner, Jr., Vice-Chairman House Committee on Science, Space and Technology, to John D. Holdren, Director of the White House Office of Science and Technology Policy, March 1, 2012, http://http://sensenbrenner.house.gov/UploadedFiles/Letter_to_John_Holdren.pdf; and U.S. Congress, Senate Committee on Homeland Security and Governmental Affairs, *Biological Security: The Risk of Dual-Use Research*, 112th Cong., 2nd sess., April 26, 2012.

[66] Examples of contracts containing prepublication review being offered by federal funding agencies is found in Peg Brickley, "Contract Conflicts," *The Scientist*, January 7, 2003; D. Malakoff, "Universities Review Policies for Onsite Classified Research," *Science*, Vol 295 (February 22, 2002) pp. 1438-1439; and Andy Fell, "Homeland Security Goals Create Impact: Campus Responds To Satisfy Range of New Terrorism Laws," *Dateline UCDavis*, November 22, 2002. See also American Association of Universities/Council on Government Relations, *Restrictions on Research Awards: Troublesome Clauses,* April 8, 2004.

[67] See, for example, AAU/COGR/NASULGC Letter to OSTP Director on Scientific Openness, found online at http://www.aau.edu/research/Ltr1.31.03.pdf.

[68] Philip Cohen, "Recipes For Bioterror: Censoring Science," *NewScientist.com*, January 18, 2003; Paul Elias, "Academic Freedoms Said Hindered by 9/11," *Washington Post*, September 11, 2003; and Gerald L. Epstein, "Preventing Biological Weapon Development Through the Governance of Life Science Research," *Biosecurity and Bioterrorism: Biodfense Strategy, Practice, and Science*, vol. 10, no. 1 (2012).

[69] "Biowarfare Warning," *Journal of the American Medical Association*, Vol. 285, No. 6 February 14, 2001, p. 725.

[70] Gerald L. Epstein, "Preventing Biological Weapon Development Through the Governance of Life Science Research," *Biosecurity and Bioterrorism: Biodfense Strategy, Practice, and Science*, vol. 10, no. 1 (2012), p. 30.

[71] National Science Advisory Board for Biosecurity, *Findings and Recommendations,* March 29-30, 2012, p. 6, http://www.nih.gov/about/director/03302012_NSABB_Recommendations.pdf.

[72] R.A. Zilinskas and J.B. Tucker, "Limiting the Contribution of the Open Scientific Literature to the Biological Weapons Threat," *Journal of Homeland Security*, (December 2002).

[73] Massachusetts Institute of Technology, *In The Public Interest. Report of the Ad Hoc Faculty Committee on Access to and Disclosure of Scientific Information*, June 2002.

[74] Percentages presented for 2009. Mark Boroush, National Science Foundation, *U.S. R&D Spending Suffered a RareDecline in 2009 but Outpaced the Overall Economy*, NSF 12-310, March 2012.

[75] Carrie Wolinetz, "Implementing the New U.S. Dual-Use Policy," *Science*, vol. 336 (June 22, 2012), pp. 1525-1527.

[76] Bruce Schneier, "Securing Medical Research: A Cybersecurity Point of View," *Science*, vol. 336 (June 22, 2012), pp. 1527-1529. Carrie Wolinetz, "Implementing the New U.S. Dual-Use Policy," *Science*, vol. 336 (June 22, 2012), pp. 1525-1527.

[77] Bruce Alberts, "H5N1," *Science*, vol. 336 (June 22, 2012), p. 1524.

[78] John Steinbruner, Elisa D. Harris, and Nancy Gallagher, et al., *Controlling Dangerous Pathogens: A Prototype Protective Oversight System*, The Center for International and Security Studies at Maryland, the University of Maryland, College Park, MD, March 2007, http://www.cissm.umd.edu/papers/files/pathogens_project_monograph.pdf.

[79] Peg Brickley, "Science Police Needed?", *The Scientist*, April 8, 2003.

[80] For more information on the Select Agent Program, see online at http://www.cdc.gov/od/sap/.

[81] Richard H. Ebright, "Mitigate the risks of release," *Nature*, vol. 481 (January 15, 2012), pp. 257-259.

[82] Public Health Agency of Canada, "Biosafety Advisory: Efficiently Transmissible Engineered Influenza A H5N1Viruses," February 1, 2012, http://www.phac-aspc.gc.ca/lab-bio/res/advi-avis/sbn-asb-2012-01-31-eng.php.

INDEX

E

I

J

K

L

M

N

Q

R

S

T

U

V

W

Y